D1327713

TIME IS MONEY
SAVE IT

TIME IS MONEY
SAVE IT

Lothar J. Seiwert

Translated by Edward J. Zajac and Linda I. Zajac

Dow Jones-Irwin
Homewood, Illinois 60430

Project editor: Suzanne Ivester
Production manager: Carma W. Fazio
Compositor: Weimer Typesetting Company, Inc.
Typeface: 11/13 Century Schoolbook
Printer: R. R. Donnelley & Sons Company

Library of Congress Cataloging-in-Publication Data

Seiwert, Lothar.
    [Mehr zeit für das wesentliche. English]
    Time is money : save it / Lothar J. Seiwert ; translated by Edward
J. Zajac and Linda I. Zajac.
      p.   cm.
    Translation of: Mehr zeit für das wesentliche.
    Includes index.
    ISBN 1-55623-185-7
    1. Time management.   I. Title.
HD69.T54S4513   1989
650.1—dc19   89–1166
                                           CIP

Printed in the United States of America

1 2 3 4 5 6 7 8 9 0 DO 6 5 4 3 2 1 0 9

FOREWORD

Do you have enough time? Your answer to this question will probably be an emphatic no. And you're in good company; approximately 90 percent of the work force replies the same way.

Time doesn't cost anything, and each of us has about the same amount at his or her disposal. But time is also one of the most precious things. It's irreplaceable; once you use time incorrectly or not at all, it's irretrievably lost.

If you successfully use the time you have at your disposal, you can solve lots of problems, decrease stress, and develop a new, confident lifestyle. To achieve this, however, you need to efficiently allocate your time and systematize your habits. You can learn to do both with a little self-discipline.

This book will show you ways to achieve your goals: to have time for the essentials—creative work, management responsibilities, and last but not least, for your private life and your family.

Klaus Jochen Schaeffer
Time/System International

CONTENTS

Introduction: How to Manage Yourself—with a Method 1

Why Self-Management? 1

Taking Stock of Your Time—Analyzing Your Current Work Habits 5

Function of Self-Management (Diagram) 15

Objective of This Book (Agreement between Reader and Author) 18

1. Goals: How to Plan Your Life and Career 22

   1.1 Function/Importance of Goals 22

   1.2 Establishing Your Goals 24

   1.3 Situation Analysis 33

   1.4 Expressing/Formulating Your Goals 40

   1.5 Summary and Analysis 42

2. Planning: How to Prepare to Carry Out Your Tasks 45

   2.1 Basics of Planning 45

   2.2 Principles and Rules of Time Planning 49

   2.3 System for Time Planning 55

   2.4 Time Planning (Daily Plans) with the Five-Step Method 62

   2.5 Management with a Time Planner 72

   2.6 Summary and Analysis 75

3. Decision Making: How to Invoke Hidden Energies and Free Up Your Time 78

   3.1 The Importance of Decision Making 79

   3.2 The Pareto Time Principle (80:20 Rule) 81

3.3	Setting Priorities through the ABC Analysis	82
3.4	A Quick Analysis according to the Eisenhower Principle	86
3.5	Understanding Delegation	88
3.6	Basic Rules of Delegation	93
3.7	Summary and Analysis	100
4.	Actualizing and Organizing: How to Take Charge of Your Daily Activities	104
4.1	Principles of Organization	105
4.2	Our Natural Daily Rhythm (the Productivity Curve)	116
4.3	Management by Biorhythm	121
4.4	Your Personal Work Style—How to Free Up Your Time	126
4.5	Your Daily Organizer	132
4.6	Summary and Analysis	134
5.	Controlling: How to Successfully Implement Your Plans	137
5.1	Functions of Controlling	137
5.2	Controlling Routines (Processes)	139
5.3	Controlling Results	142
5.4	Looking Back on Your Day (Self-Control)	143
5.5	Summary and Analysis	144
6.	Information and Communication: How Best to Deal with Meetings, Telephone Calls, and Correspondence	146
6.1	Importance of Information and Communication	147
6.2	Efficient Reading	148
6.3	Efficient Meetings	164
6.4	Efficient One-on-One Conversations—How to Manage Visitors	170
6.5	How to Be Efficient on the Phone	178
6.6	Efficient Correspondence	193
6.7	Streamlining Your Work with Checklists and Standardized Forms	198
6.8	Summary and Analysis	201
7.	Transferring: How to Put Theory into Practice	207
7.1	Looking Backward and Forward	208
7.2	Making a Contract with Yourself	209

7.3   Tips for Putting Theory into Practice   210

7.4   Avoidance Strategies and Resistance   212

7.5   Exercise   214

Works in English about Time Management   215

Index   219

TIME IS MONEY
SAVE IT

INTRODUCTION:

HOW TO MANAGE
YOURSELF—WITH A METHOD

Nothing is easier than being busy
and nothing more difficult than being effective. . . .

R. Alec Mackenzie, The Time Trap

WHY SELF-MANAGEMENT?

"Where did the time go?" is a cry frequently heard by managers under stress. We all know the problem, with more and more people encountering stress, overwork, and the pressure of time at work. Not only overwork, but lack of time planning forces managers to spend 60 hours or more at their desks.

Managers are often put under stress, since too many of their tasks are overlapping. Too many things have to be dealt with simultaneously. The result: the wrong tasks are given priority, less important tasks are not delegated; the managers' actions are ruled by the daily schedule and they are sidetracked by unimportant matters.

What Does Self-Management Mean?
To self-manage means to effectively and consistently apply appropriate working techniques on a daily basis, in order to organize ("manage") your life by using your time in the best possible way.

The principle of self-management is to consciously control your life (self-control), and not be the tool of your professional and personal environment (other-control).

The methods discussed in this book will help you to develop your professional and personal goals. This book will stress the professional part of your life. What we first want to achieve is to change your situation from one that is unplanned and externally determined to one that is goal-oriented and systematically planned.

Through efficiently allocating your time and systematizing your work methods, you will be able to get a better grip on your activities, even if you are faced with an array of diverse tasks and questions. You will be even able to *gain* time—for leisure or true management!

Sailors have an old saying, "It doesn't matter in what direction the wind blows, it's important how *I* set the sails!" Too many managers are concerned with activities (i.e., efficiency) rather than goals (i.e., effectiveness), as the following chart will show you:

Activity-Oriented (Efficiency)	*versus*	Goal-Oriented (Effectiveness)
Many managers prefer to:		
Do things right	instead of	doing the right things.
Solve problems	instead of	creating alternatives.
Save means	instead of	make the best of means.
Fulfill duties	instead of	getting results.
Reduce costs	instead of	increasing profits.

The self-management questionnaire on page 3 will allow you to analyze your current work habits. Don't be discouraged if your results are lower than 20 points, but use your energy to eliminate your weak points. This is already the first step towards self-management. (The aspects dealt with in questions 1–10 will be discussed in later chapters.)

Start Improving Your Own Situation. It is simpler, more realistic, and more successful. You don't have to convince others of the advantages of your actions and methods. You yourself will work better and more efficiently.

Self-Management: How Well Do You Master Your Work?

Self-Evaluation:

1. Before each work day I reserve a part of it for preparations and planning.
   (0) rarely   (1) sometimes   (2) often   (3) almost always
2. I delegate everything that can be delegated.
   (0) rarely   (1) sometimes   (2) often   (3) almost always
3. I write down my tasks, goals, and deadlines.
   (0) rarely   (1) sometimes   (2) often   (3) almost always
4. I try to work on each document only once and fully.
   (0) rarely   (1) sometimes   (2) often   (3) almost always
5. Each day I establish a list of tasks to be tackled, in order of their priority. I work on the most important matters first.
   (0) rarely   (1) sometimes   (2) often   (3) almost always
6. I try to keep my work day free of interrupting telephone calls, unannounced visitors, and suddenly called meetings.
   (0) rarely   (1) sometimes   (2) often   (3) almost always
7. I try to arrange my daily work according to my performance graph.
   (0) rarely   (1) sometimes   (2) often   (3) almost always
8. There is leeway in my time plan to provide for pressing or sudden matters.
   (0) rarely   (1) sometimes   (2) often   (3) almost always
9. I try to arrange my activities so that I can concentrate on the essential few problems first.
   (0) rarely   (1) sometimes   (2) often   (3) almost always
10. I can say no if others want to take up my time and I have more important things to do.
    (0) rarely   (1) sometimes   (2) often   (3) almost always

Evaluation:

Adding up the points from the analysis of your work method suggests:

Self-Management—*Concluded*

0–15 points: You have no time planning and you let yourself be influenced by others. You could, however, achieve some of your goals, if you use a priority list.

16–20 points: You try to gain control of your time, but you're not consistent enough to be successful.

21–25 points: Your self-management is good.

26–30 points: You're a model for everyone who wants to learn how to deal with time. Let others benefit from your experience!

Here are 10 advantages of self-management:

1. Finishing tasks with less waste of time.
2. Improving the organization of your own work.
3. Getting better results.
4. Being less frantic and stressful.
5. Attaining greater satisfaction with your work.
6. Generating higher motivation.
7. Increasing your qualifications for more difficult tasks.
8. Facing less pressure to work and succeed.
9. Making fewer mistakes while finishing your tasks.
10. Gaining better results at work and in your private life.

Your biggest advantage is that you will control your most precious and important resource—your time!

If You Don't Have Time, Work with This Book to Gain More Time. By consistently using the individual chapters you will learn to:

- Use the given time effectively.
- Think of and work with goals.
- Decrease stress through planning.
- Have daily results and gain at least one hour more free time a day ("the golden hour").

What do you want to do with the time you saved?

-
-
-
-

TAKING STOCK OF YOUR TIME—ANALYZING YOUR CURRENT WORK HABITS

In order to be able to change your personal work habits you have to know where your precious time goes, and, in detail, what you do and how you do it. We usually have a false perception of how we use time during the day.

Take stock of your time for a period of several days in order to analyze your current work habits and to find the reasons for any bad work habits. This step is indispensable!

A "wrong" or inefficient work method often has several causes. These include being unaware of:

- How you use time.
- How much time certain tasks require.
- The strong and weak points of your current work habits.
- The persons or circumstances that inhibit or increase your performance.

Only if you keep track of how much time you spend, with whom, and how, will you be able to discover weak points of your personal work habits and take the first step toward self-management.

Take Time

Take time to think
It is the source of power
Take time to play
It is the secret of perpetual youth
Take time to read
It is the fountain of wisdom.

Take time to pray
It is the greatest power on earth.
Take time to love and be loved
It is a God-given privilege.
Take time to be friendly
It is the road to happiness
Take time to laugh
It is the music of the soul.
Take time to give
It is too short a day to be selfish.
Take time to work
It is the price of success.
Take time to do charity
It is the key to Heaven.

Old Irish saying

We propose the following three-step method to take stock of your time:

Taking Stock of Your Time

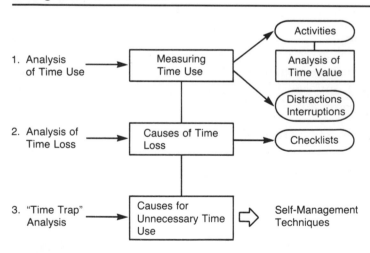

1. Analysis of Time Use

The first step is to take stock of all activities in which you play an active part. The following worksheets will help you analyze time and activities as well as distractions and interruptions.

On three or more average work days of next week, carefully and completely fill out these worksheets. Please be as honest and self-critical as possible, even if you think that the results will be disappointing. Don't deceive yourself. Only an honest analysis—for your personal use only—will show clearly where to start improving your work habits.

A.   Analysis of Time and Activities

No.	Activity	From—To	Duration (in min.)	A*	B*	C*	D*

* Do not fill in yet.

B.   Distractions and Interruptions

No.	Distraction (from—to)	Duration (in min.)	Telephone or Visitor	Who	Notes (e.g., cause for disturbances)

Instructions for Measuring Your Time Use
Equally as important as taking stock of your time is choosing typical work days. If necessary, choose a whole week as an observation period.

Try to write down everything immediately, rather than writing things down later from memory (the greatest gains from your time analysis will be lost otherwise).

Re: Work Sheet "Analysis of Time and Activities."
Confine yourself to the essentials, and register the results of all activities in 15-minute intervals.

Do not fill in the A,B,C,D slots yet. You will need them for the following analysis of activities.

Re: Worksheet "Distractions and Interruptions." Here fill in *all* distractions and interruptions that interfere with your planned or according-to-plan executed activities, including phone calls, unannounced visitors, and maybe even waiting periods.

Especially note *who* interrupted you:

  B = Boss, supervisor
Co = Colleague
Cw = Co-worker
 Se = Secretary
 Cl = Client
Su = Supplier, contractor
  F = Family
  O = Other

Keep in mind to note not only **external influences** but also if **you** yourself are the source of interruption, for example, if you—during an important activity—spontaneously pick up the phone because you remembered you have to call Mr. XYZ.

Two Approaches to Your Time Analysis

Before you start analyzing the worksheets, you should know how to evaluate the results. You can emphasize the **positive** or the **negative** aspects.

Analysis of Strong Points. All managers already use a number of successful work techniques. Otherwise they wouldn't be able to accomplish all the tasks confronting them on a daily basis. In other words, you are already a specialist in self-management techniques. Therefore, try to become aware of the strong points and advantages of your personal work method, and try to systematically improve them. Systematically apply already familiar principles of self-management on a daily basis.

Analysis of Weak Points.   As soon as you have become aware of your weak points, you can develop strategies and approaches to correct or remove them. Let this book help and advise you.

Evaluation of the Analysis of Time and Activities

After you have written down all your activities for several days, you can now analyze each worksheet and your daily work schedule using the following pattern:

1. Evaluate each activity according to the following criteria:
   A. Was the activity necessary? *Yes/No*
      (If *No*, put down *No* also under B, C, and D)
   B. Was the amount of time spent justified? *Yes/No*
   C. Did the activity serve a purpose? *Yes/No*
   D. Was the activity done at the right time? *Yes/No*
   Put down *Y* or *N* under each activity in each column.
2. Find out how much time you spend in activities during the whole day (ΣAT).
3. In each column sum up the amount of time spent with activities, that you rated No (ΣA_N, ΣB_N, ΣC_N, ΣD_N).
4. Calculate the following ratios:
   a. $\dfrac{\Sigma A_N}{\Sigma AT}$ 100%

      If more than 10 percent of activities were not completed, you have problems delegating and setting priorities (see Chapter 3).
   b. $\dfrac{\Sigma B_N}{\Sigma AT}$ 100%

      If in more than 10 percent of the cases you spent too much time, you will have to examine more closely the reasons (work habits, concentration, self-discipline, and so forth, see Chapters 2 and 4).
   c. $\dfrac{\Sigma C_N}{\Sigma AT}$ 100%

      If more than 10 percent of the activities were executed ineffectively, you will have to focus on planning and self-rationalization (see Chapters 4 and 6).

d. $\dfrac{\Sigma D_N}{\Sigma AT}$ 100%

If in more than 10 percent of all cases you chose the wrong time, you have problems planning and organizing your work time (for example, organizing your day, productivity curve, preparing your work, et cetera, see Chapters 4 and 5).

Taking stock of your time is the key to successful self-management! The method of writing everything down produces a higher learning effect and greater self-knowledge.

Evaluating the Worksheet "Disturbances and Interruptions"

Here you will try to find the causes for these interruptions.

Questions:

- What disturbances and interruptions were the most costly?
- What telephone calls were unnecessary?
- Which visitors were indispensable?
- What telephone calls could have been shorter and more effective?
- Which visits could have been shorter and more effective?
- Who (or what) caused the most, the gravest, and the most unnecessary interruptions?

What could you do *immediately?* For example, could you perhaps ask a staff member to come to you once a day and not five times a day with all his or her questions?

Make him or her prepare these daily encounters, for example, with the help of conference checklists (see also Chapter 6.3). This way, you force him or her to prepare precise questions, and you remind him or her *in advance* to have the necessary documents at hand.

2. Analysis of Time Loss

With the help of the two worksheets Analysis of Time and Activities and Distractions and Interruptions, you will now find out in detail what are your troublesome habits and what in your personal work method causes the most mistakes.

Using the following 50-point checklist to analyze your work method you will find out in what areas you are losing time or are likely to do so.

CHECKLIST
Analysis of Time Loss

Questions to Ask Yourself	Yes/No

Losing Time-Setting Objectives

1. Do I have a systematic overview of my specific work area (for example, with an Activities Checklist)? _____
2. Do I sufficiently understand the correlations between work I do and that of the company? _____
3. Do I have to accomplish too many tasks? _____
4. Am I occupied with too many different problems and tasks? _____
5. Do I manage my staff through precise objectives (Management by Objectives)? _____
6. Do I make an effort to develop new ideas and expand my knowledge and abilities on a regular basis? _____

Losing Time in the Planning Process

7. Do I know what percentage of all tasks are expected tasks? _____
8. Am I prepared for possible difficulties while working on a task? _____
9. Do I reserve some time for unexpected cases, crises, and interruptions? _____
10. Do I take precautions against disturbances in order to work uninterruptedly?
11. Do I go out on business or on business trips too often? _____
12. Do I record appointments, tasks, and activities in my daily planner? _____

Losing Time in the Decision-Making Process

13. Do I size up my work before starting with it (is the task worth the effort)? _____
14. Do I make a priority list of tasks according to their importance (e.g., A,B,C)? _____
15. Do I give the right amount of time to each task, according to importance and urgency? _____
16. Do I spend too much time with telephone calls, visitors, and conferences that are of marginal or no importance to me? _____
17. Do I try to be perfect even with matters of insignificant or secondary importance? _____
18. Do I spend too much time with routine work? _____

CHECKLIST—*Continued*

Questions to Ask Yourself	*Yes/No*

19. Do I focus too much on details in performing a task, although I already know what's important to me? _____
20. Do I have too many private conversations during work? _____

Losing Time in Organizing Work

21. Do I spend too much time with one problem, so that my performance decreases? _____
22. Do I tend toward taking on all the work myself? _____
23. Do I have co-workers or helpers to whom I could delegate appropriate tasks? _____
24. Is my desk permanently cluttered? _____
25. Do I take advantage of modern appliances that will facilitate my work (dictaphone, automatic-dial telephone, forms, checklists, etc.)? _____
26. Do I make an effort to systematically simplify the work in my area? _____
27. Do I repeatedly encounter the same difficulties in the same area? _____

Losing Time in Starting Work

28. Do I plan my workday the evening before? _____
29. Do I chat with colleagues or secretaries before starting my work? _____
30. Do I start with personal matters first? _____
31. Do I start with reading newspapers and/or the mail? _____
32. Do I need time to get back into work? _____
33. Do I take on a task spontaneously, without having thought about it? _____
34. Do I sufficiently prepare my activities? _____
35. Do I often put off important things? _____
36. Do I solve problems by starting in the middle or at the end? _____
37. Do I start certain tasks only to leave them unfinished? _____

Losing Time Planning Your Day

38. Do I know my personal work rhythm and productivity rhythm? _____
39. Do I know whether I perform better in the morning or at night? _____
40. Does my workday correspond with my productivity rhythm? _____
41. Do I plan to work the time of day when I work best? _____
42. At these peak hours, am I occupied with routine work, matters of insignificance, or secondary importance? _____

Losing Time in the Information and Communication Process

43. Do I choose reading material of importance and usability? _____
44. Do I skim over my reading material in order to grasp the main ideas and later read in detail? _____

CHECKLIST—*Concluded*

Questions to Ask Yourself	Yes/No

45. Do I end a telephone call, conversation, or conference, when continuing it is unnecessary? _____
46. Am I sufficiently prepared for meetings? _____
47. Do I make sure I know what my conversation partner and I want to achieve in order to save energy and time? _____
48. Do I prepare my correspondence with simple or detailed notes? _____
49. Do I avoid taking notes that I would only need in the most unlikely of situations? _____
50. Do I use forms for routine tasks? _____

What Are Your Results? Don't be discouraged if you checked a lot of weak points! After you analyzed your current work method you will be able to follow the chapters in this book with a higher awareness: all the above mentioned problems will be dealt with there.

List All Your Problem Spots according to Priority! That way you'll make sure you can work through the following chapters systematically.

Most Frequent Sources of Time Loss
1.
2.
3.
4.
5.
6.
7.
8.
9.
10.

3. Time Waster Analysis

Finally, try to identify your own five most frequent and major sources of time loss!

From the following list of the 30 most important "time-eaters" or "time wasters," pick those five that are most consequential for you:

1. Objectives unclear
2. No priorities
3. Taking on too many tasks at a time
4. Lack of overview of future tasks and activities
5. Insufficient planning of the day
6. Personal disorganization/cluttered desk
7. Paperwork and reading
8. Inadequate filing system
9. Searching for notes, addresses/telephone numbers
10. Lack of motivation/indifference toward work
11. Lack of coordination/teamwork
12. Phone interrupts
13. Unannounced visitors
14. Inability to say no
15. Incomplete, belated information
16. Lack of self-discipline
17. Not finishing a task
18. Distractions and noise
19. Lengthy meetings
20. Insufficient preparation for meetings and conferences
21. No or imprecise communication
22. Private chatting
23. Too much communication
24. Too many notes
25. Procrastination
26. Wanting to know all the facts
27. Waiting time (e.g., at appointments)
28. Haste, impatience
29. Not enough delegation
30. Insufficient control over delegated tasks

Keep in mind that in fighting your most frequent time wasters you're already on your way toward significantly improving productivity. This book will provide a wide range of suggestions of how to approach the various problems.

No one knows your personal work problems better than you do, so this is the time to start practicing *active self-*

management: make an outline of the causes for your time wasters and ways to solve these problems:

Time Wasters	Possible Causes	Solutions, Ideas

Complete the list while working through each of the chapters.

FUNCTION OF SELF-MANAGEMENT (DIAGRAM)

We might visualize the mastering of day-to-day tasks and problems as a sequence of interconnected activities.

This process of self-management may be depicted in the following diagram showing the interrelations of all functions of self-management.

There are five different functions in the outer circle:

1. Setting an objective:
   Analysis and definition of personal goals.
2. Planning:
   Making up plans and alternatives for your own activities.
3. Decision making:
   Making decisions on prospective tasks.
4. Implementing:
   Structuring and organizing of daily personal work flow in order to put tasks into action.
5. Control:
   Self-control and control of results (and, if need be change of the objective).

The inner circle shows the complementary function.

6. Information and communication:
   The other functions in a way "revolve" around this because communication as exchange of information is in-

dispensable for each of the activities in the self-management process.

Diagram of Self-Management

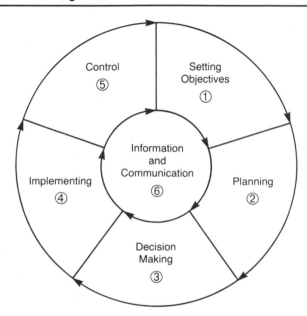

The sequence of the above functions is not as simple as shown in this diagram, but the functions are interrelated in numerous ways. The illustrations in the chapters of this book will point out work techniques and methods relevant for each of the self-management functions. They will also show you how to apply them (see the following table).

Table of Systematic Self-Management Techniques

Function = Chapter	Working Techniques Methods	Successes, Results (gaining time through:)

1. Setting objectives	Setting an objective
	Analyzing the situation
	Objective strategies and
	  successful methods
	Defining the objective
		Motivation
		Elimination of weak
		  points
		Recognizing advantages
		Concentrating energy on
		  bottlenecks
		Writing down appoint-
		ments and next steps

Table of Systematic Self-Management Techniques—*Concluded*

Function = Chapter	Working Techniques Methods	Successes, Results (gaining time through:)

2. Planning	Yearly
	Monthly
	Weekly
	Daily planning
	Principles of time-
	  management
	Five-step method
	Using a time planner
		Preparing to set
		  objectives into action
		Optimal distribution and
		  utilization of
		  discretionary time
		Reducing time needed
		  for performance

3. Decision making	Setting priorities
	Pareto time principle
	  (80:20 rule)
	ABC analysis
	Eisenhower principle
	Delegating
		Successful arrangement
		  of work
		Essential problems have
		  priority over problems
		  of secondary
		  importance
		Arranging tasks in order
		  of priority (importance)
		Overcoming the
		  "tyranny" of pressing
		  issues
		Productive management
		  of personnel

4. Implementing	Arranging the day
	Productivity curve
	Biorhythm
	Self-development
	Daily framework
		Applying self-
		  management
		Concentrating on
		  essential tasks
		Making use of
		  productivity peaks
		Considering periodic
		  fluctuation
		Developing a personal
		  work style

5. Control	Controlling the work flow
	  (actual versus
	  expected comparison)
	Controlling results
	  (means, ends, and in-
	  between)
	Looking back on the day
	  (self-control)
		Ensuring planned
		  performance
		Positive lifestyle

6. Information and
  communication
	Effective reading
	Effective meetings
	Effective face-to-face
	  communication (visitor
	  management)
	Effective correspondence
	Checklists, forms
		Reading faster
		Organizing conferences
		  more effectively
		Office hours
		Screening from
		  disturbances
		Fewer interruptions
		Less paperwork

OBJECTIVE OF THIS BOOK (AGREEMENT BETWEEN READER AND AUTHOR)

By now you have taken the self-management test—I hope—and you are familiar with the possibilities and problems of monitoring your time. Maybe you have also already gone through the 50-question-checklist Analysis of Time Loss, and the result should read: you can absolutely become a better self-manager—*if you want to!*

You will already be familiar with most of the time-management techniques and work methods introduced in this book. But the compact and systematic arrangement of ideas will be new to you. However, the main problem of all work methods lies somewhere else: in their consistent use and transfer into practice.

What I, as the author, *don't* want you to do is:

- To put the book aside after you've read it.
- To start with one method or the other, and—after a while—to notice that all good intentions were lost in the daily demands of work.

And I don't think that *you* want that either!

Therefore, I'd like to make a contract with you—just like computer manufacturers who are marketing their hardware and software (here it is the price of the book!) Computer companies also don't want you to not use their products!

If you feel this is unnecessary—if you don't want to make an agreement for the time you're reading this book—then you run the risk of outwitting yourself—once again. You may decide not to take any responsibility for changes (i.e., improvements) in your work methods and habits. As a result, after reading the book and attempting to put into effect some of its suggestions, you may come up with a negative judgment and say to yourself, "None of this works anyway—there's no point to these work methods and self-management ideas. I might have known that they wouldn't work out!" Then you can make whatever use you want of this "discomforting" book that invites you to make contractual agreements on how to use it and how to change your work habits (see Chapter 7). You might decide to just decorate your bookshelf with it—but bear in mind that you made a commitment in purchasing this book!

For this is a discomforting book—it's a *workbook* that demands your full cooperation and your readiness to critically question your work habits and time-planning techniques and to change them. It's worth the effort!

Ask yourself again: What did I really have in mind when I bought this book?

-
-
-

What can I do to get where I want to be?

-
-
-

What did I do in similar situations (reading a textbook, taking part in a seminar, etc.), where I got little or nothing out of them?
How did I deceive myself?

-
-
-

How did I feel afterward?

-
-
-

What do I want to do differently this time in order to reach my goal?

-
-
-

Contract between Reader and Author

Date: _____

1. What do I really want to achieve? (Try to be as precise as possible!)

2. What do I want to do to achieve that (time and energy that I'm willing to invest)?

3. When do I want to start?

4. For how long am I willing to try?

5. How often do I want to work on my daily self-management (e.g., half an hour/one hour each day)?

6. Whom do I want to involve (secretary, staff, colleague, partner)?

7. What could I possibly do to deceive myself in order not to fulfill the contract?

8. What other difficulties are to be expected (e.g., hectic environment in the company)?

9. Date of first audit to see whether I kept the contract (after one to two weeks).

Now ask yourself: • What was the reason?
• Do I really want that?
• How can I change it?

_____   _____
Reader   Author

If you (allegedly) don't have time to work on your self-management, take the time now to have more time later! To illustrate, here's a little story. *Please, don't read it.*

> A hiker was strolling through a wood, when he met a lumberjack, who hastily and arduously was trying to saw a felled tree trunk into little pieces. The hiker came closer to see why the lumberjack was struggling so hard, and he said, "Excuse me, but I just noticed: your saw is totally blunt! Don't you want to sharpen it?"
>
> The lumberjack groaned, "I don't have time for that—I have to saw!"

Did you read it anyway? When do *you* want to sharpen your saw?

CHAPTER 1

GOALS: HOW TO PLAN YOUR LIFE AND CAREER

After we'd definitely lost sight of our goal,
we doubled our efforts.

Mark Twain

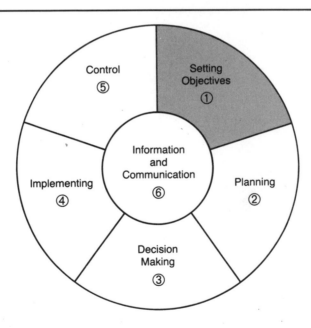

1.1 FUNCTION/IMPORTANCE OF GOALS

Setting goals means: (1) to intend to put into action and put into words our needs, interests, desires, or tasks; and (2) to direct our actions toward these goals and their realization.

Every company has goals. Since we are dealing with personal management, we are going to take a closer look at the importance of goals in your area. Setting goals means to look into the future, directing and concentrating energy and activities on those goals. Goals thus already lead to results. It doesn't matter what you do but what goal you have in mind. Goals are challenging and an incentive for action. Without goals every activity and every result is right—or wrong. You are lacking the criterion to measure your efforts. If you haven't clearly established your goals ahead of time, even the best work method will be useless. Objectives provide the incentives and act as motivators for our actions.

Objectives are projections into the future. You have to work to make them real. Otherwise intentions are all that is left. Traditional thinking about individual tasks leads to getting lost in details. Thinking about goals makes you see the individual task as part of a bigger project: you know where to go and what results to get.

During your daily activities you have to ask yourself continuously: Can I reach my goal by doing what I am doing right now?

Setting goals is a permanent process, since goals aren't static but can change constantly; e.g., if you realize that your perceptions were wrong or your demands too high or too low (see the management diagram on page 22). Setting goals means to consciously direct your actions along certain principles. It is fundamental for self-management and a conscious lifestyle to know where we want to go and where we don't want to go (self-determination), and not where others want us to go (heteronomy). If I am consciously setting goals, my unconscious energy is automatically concentrated on my actions. Goals help us focus our energy. To know your objectives and to pursue them with determination is helpful in using all your energy to deal with important matters instead of wasting it on unimportant matters. To realize your own goals can also be an enormous self-motivation in your own work.

Accidental success is good, but rare. Planned success is better, happens more often, and can be influenced. A prerequisite of planning—and success—is to know exactly: what you want to achieve, when, and to what extent.

Setting goals is indispensable for planning, decision making, and your daily work. If you come into your office with the attitude: "I'm going to work on whatever is pressing," stop it right now! Set clear goals for yourself (and your staff) and work according to the principle: "I'm going to work on my goals today!"

This chapter follows the process of setting objectives:

Setting Goals

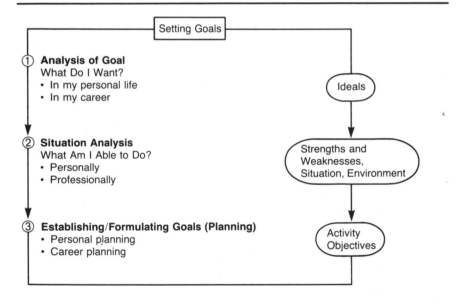

1.2 ESTABLISHING YOUR GOALS

You want to be more successful—otherwise you wouldn't have bought this book. To achieve something and to be successful you have to expend time and effort. Careful planning is necessary to achieve the goals you wish to achieve within an appropriate period of time:

- What are your objectives?
- What do they look like? Are they compatible?
- Are there main objectives and intermediate objectives on your way there?
- Do you know what you are able to do (strengths) and what you will still have to work on (weaknesses)?

Know Your Goals!

This is an indispensable, basic prerequisite for successfully planning your life and work. To find and define personal goals means to give your life direction and to be able to realize your ideals. Try to define goals that can be put into direct action.

Examples:

1. Wrong: I want to live healthier.
   Right: I will jog 30 minutes each day.
2. Wrong: I want to have a better relationship with my staff.
   Right: I will reserve one hour per week for each staff member to discuss professional and private issues.

You can reserve time on certain days or weeks for these precise objectives in a time planner, and after that put them into action.

Therefore, Write Down Exactly What You Want to Achieve!

When you write, vague ideas become more concrete. In recording your goals you are forced to critically review them and to state them more precisely. Through visualization goals are less easily forgotten. If you establish your goals in writing, they automatically become more binding: if you put down your goals on paper, you will have to deal with them, review them. With the help of several exercises in this section we want you to think about your objectives, to find precise issues, to systematize them and write them down.

From Ideals to Objectives:
You can find or establish your personal objectives by following these four steps:

1. Establish your personal ideal in life.
2. List your ideals chronologically.
3. Establish your career ideal.
4. Establish an inventory of objectives.

1.   Establish Your Personal Ideal in Life

Imagine what your future life could look like. Don't be upset over failures and defeats in the past: you can't change them anymore—but you can learn from them!

Preparation: My Life Curve
- What has my life been like so far?
- What were my biggest successes? Defeats? Professionally? Personally?
- What do I want my future to look like?
- How old do I want to get?
- What do I still want to achieve?
- What misfortunes or defeats do I expect to face?

Draw your life curve on the following graph (the way it has gone thus far), and mark where you are today. Briefly label your successes and failures at the peaks of the curve. Try to picture your future and draw the graph accordingly.

Draw Your Life Curve

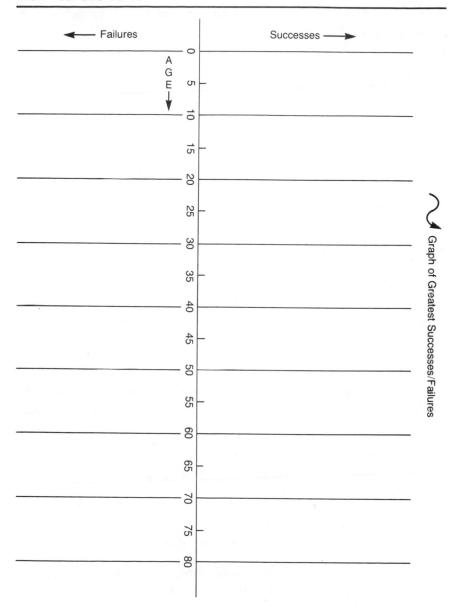

Your Personal Ideal of Life:
Name the five most important things you want to achieve in
your lifetime:

    1.
    2.
    3.
    4.
    5.

The next step:

2. List Your Ideals Chronologically

It is unimportant for now whether you see your own ideas as
realistic or utopian—this aspect will be looked into at a later
time. More important are the guidelines governing your life
and the wishes you want to realize. Even seemingly utopian
goals can act as motivators for your future work and life.

In the following exercise it is important for you to think
about what events you'll have to reckon with within the next
20 years of your personal time chart. Take into account those
people to whom you relate most closely (partner/husband-wife,
children, boss, friends, etc.), and their ages. Likely events could
be:

- Children starting school.
- Children graduating.
- Father/mother retiring.
- Supervisor retiring.
- Mortgage expiring.
- CDs or other savings becoming due.

The following time chart will show you how your personal
ideals and objectives relate to important dates of your personal
environment.

Time Chart of Personal Objectives

Year	Your Age	Age of Related Persons					Special Events
1990							
1991							
1992							
1993							
1994							
1995							
1996							
1997							
1998							
1999							
2000							
2001							
2002							
2003							
2004							
2005							
2006							
2007							

On the next chart fill in all your goals for the near and distant future:

- Long-term objectives.
  What do I want to achieve in this world, in this lifetime?

- Medium-term objectives.
  What do I want to achieve within the next five years?
- Short-term objectives.
  What do I want to achieve within the next 12 months?

Ideals and Objectives
Private objectives

- Long-term (life goals)
- Medium-term (five years)
- Short-term (within next 12 months)

Professional objectives

- Long-term (career objectives)
- Medium-term (five years)
- Short-term (within next 12 months)

In the next step toward establishing your personal goals, we want to take a closer look at the professional area:

3.   Establish Your Career Goal

What would you like to do professionally? If you could freely choose your position, function, title, industry and organization, company or institution, what would you like to be?
Examples:

- Becoming the executive of a midsize company in the XY industry.
- Being the CEO of company X or Y.
- Opening or heading a subsidiary in a foreign country (where?).
- Being regarded an expert in . . . .
- Getting tenure, get a Ph.D. or an M.B.A.
- Starting your own business.
- Starting a political career.
- Dropping out in five years and traveling around the world.

Your answer:

Professional Ideal

- I would like to be or become . . . at . . . .
- or: I would like to be or become . . . at . . . .
- or: I want to be my own boss, start my own business in . . .

Your professional ideals are the key to your professional and personal success:

- They act as strong motivators for work and energy.
- They direct your activities, orientation, and professional decisions.
- They are the guideline for your future professional work.

Review Your Ideal with the Next Exercise

Imagine your dream profession and try to reflect on it with the following questions:

- Why am I not doing it now?
  Answer:
- What have I done to eliminate the obstacles facing me?
  Answer:
- What have I done to get closer to the position I want?
  Answer:
- Do I know the requirements of the position I want?
  Answer:
- If not, to what extent am I really interested in it?
  Answer:
- What is the main problem keeping me from getting closer to the desired position?
  Answer:
- What have I done up to now to reduce or eliminate these problems?
  Answer:
- What needs to be done?
  Answer:
- What goal do I want to set for myself in order to overcome these difficulties over a specific period of time?
  Answer:

The last step in establishing your personal and professional objectives is to make an:

4.   Inventory of Objectives/Goals

Review the exercises in Steps 1–3, and make a list of your objectives. Out of this list select those objectives most important to your life and career.

Consider also those ideals or childhood dreams that could perhaps be realized through a single investment of time and money, e.g., traveling around the world, spending six months on an island in the South Pacific, etc. If you list these objectives under the category *things that I want to do,* they become more real and a basis for your future plans. Your goals become incentives to move toward action, rather than letting your goals linger on in your fantasy world for the next five or 10 years.

Inventory of Objectives
Personal goals (life goals)

-
-
-

Professional goals (career goals)

-
-
-

Experiences that I want to have:
Personal

-
-
-

Professional

-
-
-

Things I want to do:
Personal

-
-
-

Professional

-
-
-

1.3 SITUATION ANALYSIS

After you established your personal and professional goals in the prior section, we now want to focus on your personal resources—the means to achieve your goals. Again, we want to proceed in four steps:

1. Central questions for a situation analysis.
2. Personal balance sheet of successes/failures
3. Strengths and weaknesses
4. Ends-means analysis

This situation analysis will reveal your strengths and weaknesses and show the areas that you can expand or that require improvement. What can you do to positively influence your life curve?

On the next pages you will find a number of:

1. Central Questions regarding Your Personal and Professional Situation to Examine Your Present Situation

Questions regarding Your Personal Situation

My résumé: What were my greatest successes and failures?

Family influences: Childhood? Youth? Parents? Siblings? Other people close to me?

What are my strongest character traits, advantages, and strengths?

What are my weaknesses?

Where am I in harmony/conflict with my environment? What are the reasons?

Who are my friends? Enemies?

How and when do I feel strong, inferior, or weak?

Where couldn't I succeed up to now? Why?

What dangers, difficulties, problems could I face? In what areas?

What steps do I want to take here?

What people, friends, etc. further my efforts or hinder my development?

In what areas can I develop my abilities? Where not? What can I do against it?

What negative outside influences do I want to eliminate?

What positive influences do I want to exploit?

What do others need? What can I give?

Where and whom can I help? (maybe in organizations)

To whom am I useful?

What do I precisely want to do to be useful to others?

How much ransom money would I pay for my best friends?

Am I useful to those who are the most useful to me?

Whom will I please? Right now? Tomorrow?

Questions regarding Your Professional Situation
Do I know the objectives of my position?

Do I know what is expected of me?

Did I discuss my objectives with my superior?

Do I know the routine work in my area?

Do I plan my tasks?

Do I always have an overview of the tasks that are not yet accomplished?

Do I know how urgent and important my tasks are?

Do I set priorities?

Do I complete my tasks punctually?

Does that put me frequently under pressure?

Do I have to be reminded to finish my tasks?

Do I procrastinate?

Do I independently tackle tasks?

Do I carry out my tasks fully?

Do I get a lot of queries or complaints?

Do people complain about getting insufficient information from me?

To what extent does the company influence my private life?

What is my range of competence?

How useful am I in my current efforts?

What compensation can I achieve (salary, advancement, contacts, etc.)?

What kind of success will I be able to achieve in the near future?

What failures do I have to reckon with?

What are the main assets of the company?

After we found out about the "Where do I want to go?" (establishing your objectives), let's think about "Where am I?" In the next section we want to analyze your strengths and weaknesses. For that purpose I would like you to take a look at your life curve again (see p. 27), and in the following exercise to list your:

2. Greatest Personal and Professional Successes

What abilities, knowledge, and experience were necessary to achieve these successes? Try to find out what abilities you used in each of the cases:

Personal Knowledge + Abilities

Specialized knowledge

- Product knowledge
- Knowledge of the production process
- Sales techniques
- Knowledge of management techniques
- General knowledge
- Contacts and connections

Personality

- Physical fitness
- Appearance, activity, stamina
- Social skills, ability to listen, empathy
- Adaptability, helpfulness
- Ability to criticize and to take criticism

Leadership qualities

- Ability to push things through, to persuade
- Ability to delegate, instruct
- Ability to motivate people and groups
- Readiness for teamwork and cooperation

Mental abilities

- Judgment
- Creativity
- Logical thinking
- Structured, systematic thinking

Work methods

- Consistent and systematic work methods
- Decision making, problem solving
- Power of concentration, rapid/systematic reading
- Work methods, organizing
- Rhetoric, discussion and negotiating techniques

Personal Successes

My Greatest Successes, Efforts, Etc.	How Did I Achieve Them? (Necessary Abilities)
1.	
2.	
3.	
4	
5.	
6.	
7.	
8.	
9.	
10.	

By analyzing your abilities you will find out what you are able to achieve, and what personal resources are at your disposal. We must enhance these resources. But this is only one aspect. You also have to know your weaknesses, either to avoid activities that further these "skills," or to take steps to eliminate them. You therefore also have to list your greatest failures and defeats and what you might have lacked in ability, i.e., the features that might have caused them. Also try to remember how you overcame the failures at the time. To know your weaknesses means to increase your strengths!

Personal Failures

My Greatest Failures, Defeats, Etc.	Lacking Abilities	How Did I Overcome These Failures?
1.		
2.		
3.		
4.		
5.		
6.		
7.		
8.		
9.		
10.		

3.   Strengths and Weaknesses

Here you will organize your abilities and shortcomings according to area and list the two or three most important strengths and weaknesses. The resulting personal ability profile forms the basis for planning the next steps toward your goals.

Process of Goal Setting

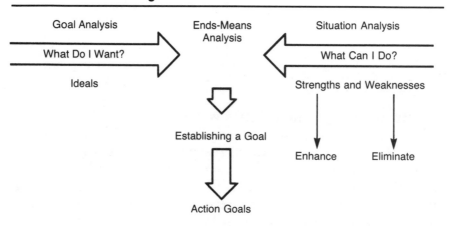

Ability Profile	Strengths +	Weaknesses −
Professional knowledge and experience	1. 2. 3.	1. 2. 3.
Social and communicative skills	1. 2. 3.	1. 2. 3.
Personal skills	1. 2. 3.	1. 2. 3.
Leadership qualities	1. 2. 3.	1. 2. 3.
Mental abilities, work methods	1. 2. 3.	1. 2. 3.
Other	1. 2. 3.	1. 2. 3.

The last step of our situation analysis is the:

4. Ends/Means Analysis

Here we will compare the status quo with the means (personal, financial, and time resources) necessary to reach our goal. Go back to Chapter 1.2. to take a look at the list of goals (inventory of goals), and pick out the five most important goals. Find out what the necessary means for their achievement are and what else you will have to do in order to achieve these goals.

Examples

Ends	Means	Available
1. Playing Robinson Crusoe on an island in the South Pacific	Six months' time $10,000 for travel Knowing how to sail and fish Knowing the language	x x
2. CEO of marketing in a subsidiary		

For career objectives, list the necessary job qualifications under the category *means,* and then derive definite, realistic goals regarding the experience and abilities you are still lacking.

Ends/Means Analysis

Ideals	Necessary Means	Situation Analysis		Objectives Measures
		Available (abilities, etc.)	Unavailable	
1.				
2.				
3.				
4.				
5.				

1.4 EXPRESSING/FORMULATING YOUR GOALS

The last step in the process of establishing objectives consists of formulating your goals and then deriving action-oriented goals for planning purposes.

Life and Career Plan
Transfer your life and career goals from the exercise charts to the following charts.

Setting Dates—Establishing Expected Results. We mentioned at the beginning of this chapter that establishing professional or personal goals makes sense only when you (1) set a definite date or point in time and (2) formulate results.

Set dates for your goals and review your plans in terms of their being realistic. You be the judge!

Consider also issues like your body and your health because good health is the basis for an active, goal-oriented life and for successful self-management. Therefore, include in your periodic plans by the year, month, and day time for activities such as cross-country skiing, swimming, jogging, yoga, etc., and routine medical checkups.

Don't forget to broaden your horizons and to further your cultural development through travel and cultural activities.

Be careful not to take on too much at one time. A burdensome task has little chance of being realized. The more goals you set for yourself, the more you'll be forced to change your life or take up new activities.

Set concrete, short-term goals that ultimately work toward more complex ones. Long-term goals often imply a changing environment and new developments. It is psychologically and motivationally important to pursue short-term goals in order to experience success.

EXAMPLE
Life Plan (Excerpt)

Area of Life	No.	Ideal Wish	Impor-tance	Target Date	Actions to Take	Deadline for Actions	Control
Property, money	4	House in desirable neighbor-hood	High	1994	Look for lot, Raise person-al capital, Sell condo w/profit	1989 1991 1993	

Life Plan

Area of Life	No.	Ideal Wish	Impor-tance	Target Date	Goals, Next Steps	Deadline for Actions	Control

Setting goals for your professional life requires researching the company, industry, and the market. Developing your personal and professional knowledge and experience plays a significant role here.

Where Could You Most Probably Be Promoted within the Next Two or Three Years?

Job description:

Area of responsibility:

Additionally needed professional skills:

Leadership qualities:

Personal skills:

Other criteria:

What Is Important for Your Career Planning? A small step that can be tackled *immediately* is better than extensive, strategic and fantastic planning for the future that will only delay actions.

What Does Your Next Step Look Like?

Goal of next step:

Necessary information:

Essential resources:

Possible difficulties, problems:

Procedure, measures:

Deadlines:

Record this next step in your career plan:

EXAMPLE
Career Plan

No.	Ideal Professional Career	Impor-tance	Target Year	Actions to Take	Deadline for Action	Control
3	Marketing director in mid-size company	High	1993	Sales experience, assistant marketing director	1989	

1.5   SUMMARY AND ANALYSIS

Thinking in objectives makes you think of the task as part of a bigger project.

- We establish objectives in three steps:
  1. Analysis of objective: What do I want?
  2. Situation analysis: What can I do? What are my capabilities?
  3. Formulating objective: What will I tackle definitely?

- Become certain about your objectives by stipulating in writing exactly what you want to achieve (life and career goals)
- In the goal inventory you will find all personal or professional ideals gradually elaborated in this chapter
- The analysis of your personal and professional situation provides you with an inventory of your personal resources needed to achieve your goals. It further explains where your strengths and weaknesses are.
- Our next step is the ends-means analysis, where you can compare the necessary personal, financial, and time resources necessary for achieving your goals with the resources already available.
- From the paragraph dealing with different steps necessary to achieve your goals (e.g., concentrating on particular strengths) you can derive definite goals to be acted upon in the future process of self-management. Formulating goals means to set deadlines and stipulate results.
- Finally we record our objectives in a life and career plan which should be reviewed, updated, and completed on a regular basis.

Now you can analyze this chapter with respect to your personal goals.

- What in particular seems to be especially important to me?
- What particular new insights did I gain?
- What did I find that confirmed my own insights?
- What area would I like to work on in detail?
- What do I want to translate into action?

Analysis of Chapter 1

Result No.	Pages	Ideas, Suggestions, Topics of Value	Target Dates for Attainment	Control

In this chapter you've analyze and established your life goals and your work objectives. In the next chapter—"Planning: How to Prepare to Carry Out Your Tasks"—we'll show you how to carry out these goals and objectives.

CHAPTER 2

PLANNING: HOW TO PREPARE TO CARRY OUT YOUR TASKS

Plan your work—work your plan!

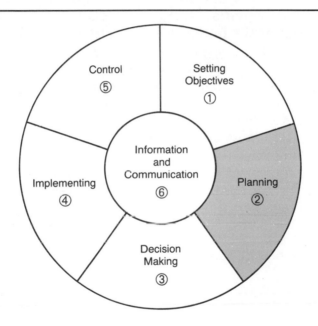

2.1 BASICS OF PLANNING

Time planning seeks to guarantee that the previous resource called *time* is used economically. This means that you either:

- Use the time at your disposal for tasks that promise the greatest reward (maximum criterion), or
- Achieve your goals within a minimum of time (minimum criterion).

The more we organize (that is, plan) our time, the better we can use it for our personal or professional ideals. Planning, according to the circle of self-management, involves:

Preparation of Task Performance

+

Time Structuring

By planning your daily, medium-term and long-term activities and events you will gain time, success, and the ability to keep calm when facing daily demands.

Since every company does plan and must plan its market or operational activities, every individual should think and work in terms of the future in his or her area, and not be led by events that just happen to come along. As an executive you know very well the advantages of business planning. Therefore, we would like to suggest the following to you: Be an entrepreneur in your specialty and plan the use of your precious time to achieve your goals!

The greatest advantage of planning is that planning time means gaining time!

Experience shows that with investing a little more time in planning you will need less time for implementation and can save time altogether:

Time for Planning	Time Needed for Implementation

Total of Invested Time

Time for Planning	Time Needed for Implementation	Time-Gain

Obviously this process can't be expanded indefinitely. After you reach an optimal point, any further time investment in planning becomes ineffective (overplanning).

Since the daily activities in a company are changing and can't be totally predicted, it is nearly impossible to plan and

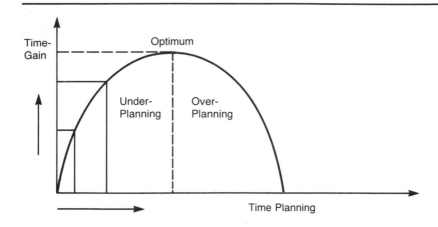

achieve the absolute optimum. But even if you gain only 30 minutes each day, planning is a success. We might make the following factual statement on this point: *Whoever invests 10 minutes in planning his or her workday can save two hours a day, and will be able to implement tasks more accurately and with better quality.*

A rule of thumb that has proven itself is: Reserve a maximum of 1 percent planning time for the time period to be planned (a year, a month, a week, a day).

Example:
Reserve approximately 5 to 10 minutes for planning a workday.

Finally, here is a list of answers to the question "Why is planning necessary?" For the first run-through please fill in today's date, and then check all the points you want to achieve:

Advantages of Time Planning in Terms of Time Management and Self-Management	Date of First Run-Through	Date of Second Run-Through
Reaching a Goal		
• Establishing personal and professional goals	_____	_____
• Achieving personal and professional goals faster and better	_____	_____
• Looking at goals realistically in terms of the shortage of time	_____	_____

Advantages of Time Planning in Terms of Time Management and Self-Management	Date of First Run-Through	Date of Second Run-Through

Gaining Time

• Saving and gaining time for essential tasks and goals (executive duties, staff, family, leisure)	_____	_____

Overview

• Chronological overview of all projects, tasks, and activities (doing what, when, and in what time frame?)	_____	_____
• Better estimation of time required to accomplish tasks	_____	_____

Priorities

• Concentrating on essential tasks and ensuring their implementation	_____	_____
• Distinguishing essential activities from less essential ones as well as the tasks to be delegated	_____	_____

Deadlines

• Realistically keeping and assessing deadlines and the time needed to attain them	_____	_____
• Becoming quickly aware of tight spots ahead and planning how to avoid them	_____	_____

Time Reserves

• Creating time buffers for unpredictable events	_____	_____

Effectiveness

• Structuring the daily schedule in advance to allow for better use of time	_____	_____
• Dividing up tasks and taking care of related tasks in blocks	_____	_____
• Avoiding idle moments for you and your staff	_____	_____

Delegation

• Having a good working relationship with your staff	_____	_____
• Delegating tasks to your staff	_____	_____

Advantages of Time Planning in Terms of Time Management and Self-Management	Date of First Run-Through	Date of Second Run-Through
• Placing orders inside and outside the company	_____	_____
Decreasing Stress		
• Striving for a less hectic, more predictable day; planning your breaks	_____	_____
• Decreasing stress by finishing more tasks	_____	_____
• Having more fun working; reducing the pressure of deadlines, frustration, and impatience	_____	_____

If, after a second run-through (see Chapter 7, "Transferring: How to Put Theory into Practice"), you have achieved three or more goals, your new time planning will be a great success—for you (and for me as the author).

2.2 PRINCIPLES AND RULES OF TIME PLANNING

You have to be aware of the fact that you have only a limited time budget for achieving your goals. Planning means projecting outlines of your future tasks for certain time periods; it means dealing more effectively with changes in your responsibilities. We do not only plan our professional and personal goals but also our recurring pressures. The better you know your time budget and your responsibilities, the better will you be prepared to delegate, to reduce the number of tasks or postpone the less important ones. We don't want you to be deterred by an abundance of rules, so pick the five principles you think most important and which you're most likely to apply:

1. Basic Principle (60:40 Rule)	*Ranking*	*Comments*
Organize only a certain percentage of your total working hours (typically 60 percent).		

To be able to deal with unforeseen events, interruptions (time wasters) and personal interests and needs, you should not plan 100 percent of your time. Therefore, you should organize your time into three blocks:

Principles of Time Planning
- Approximately 60 percent of activities planned.
- Approximately 20 percent of activities unplanned (reserve for buffers and unplanned activities).
- Approximately 20 percent for spontaneous activities (leadership tasks, creative periods).

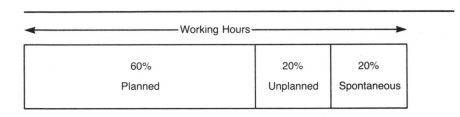

The nature of your activities will determine whether these variables will deviate upward or downward. The results of your activities and time analysis could supply you with the following information.

2. *Analysis of Time and Activities/Distractions*	*Ranking*	*Comments*
Check how you (mis-)spend your time and where (see p. 7 for checklists).		

This way you will:

- Maintain an overview of your time budget.
- Gather empirical facts as a basis for future time assessments.
- Get a starting point for improving your personal work habits and time planning (e.g., eliminating time wasters).

3. *List of Tasks/Activities*   *Ranking*   *Comments*

List *all* activities on the agenda for the time period in question. Unaccomplished tasks can be dealt with when free time comes up or can be planned into the next period's plan.

Maintaining an overview of all tasks on the agenda is important for good time planning. Divide your agenda into long-, mid-, and short-term tasks. Set and keep priorities (see No. 13 on page 53), even if less important tasks are often easier to handle than difficult, but very important tasks.

Here you can use the Activities Checklist form (see p. 59 for an example).

4. *Regularity—Consistency*   *Ranking*   *Comments*

Check your time plans regularly and systematically, and consistently finish your tasks. To follow the method and your schedules is more important than to meticulously fill out the checklists.

5. *Planning Realistically*   *Ranking*   *Comments*

Don't overplan: only plan what you can realistically accomplish.

6. *Flexibility*   *Ranking*   *Comments*

Be flexible: time plans do not exist to be followed for their own sake, but to achieve goals.

7. *Time Loss*   *Ranking*   *Comments*

If possible, try to compensate for eventual time loss immediately (e.g., stay longer one night instead of trying to make up for lost time over several days).

8. *Putting It in Writing*   *Ranking*   *Comments*

Using your own checklists or those in your appointment calendar, write down your plans. Thus you won't lose anything and you'll have a good overview.

9. *Unaccomplished Tasks*	*Ranking*	*Comments*

Transfer all unaccomplished indispensable tasks into the plan for the next
period. This keeps them visible and
automatically included in your new
plans.

10. *Results—Not Activities*	*Ranking*	*Comments*

Write down results or goals, not just
activities.

Examples:
- Don't write "Call J. Smith"—write "Discuss data processing with J. Smith."
- Don't write "Meeting with A. Kane"—write "Discuss contracts of apprentices with A. Kane."

In this way your activities will focus on certain goals, and you'll avoid unplanned activities, such as discussing irrelevant issues.

You have to ask yourself constantly: What do I want to achieve with this meeting or this activity? What is this goal?

11. *Time Frames*	*Ranking*	*Comments*

Establish precise time frames, and
plan only as much time as is actually
needed for a specific task.

For experience has shown that a task usually takes as long as time allows. For example, if you routinely plan meetings for Mondays from 10:00 A.M. to 12:00 P.M., every meeting will take that long, even if your actual goal has already been achieved. But if you plan "discussion of and deciding on sales strategies for May (90 minutes)," you're forced to stay within that precise time frame and to focus on the essentials in order to achieve your goal.

12. *Deadlines*	*Ranking*	*Comments*

Set deadlines for all your activities. In
forcing yourself toward self-discipline
you will avoid indecision, delays, and
procrastination (see also the Activities
Checklist, page 59 and Project
Management form, page 99).

Eliminate vague phrases like "as soon as possible" or "as fast as possible." What do they really mean: Within an hour? Today? Next week? Within two or three weeks?

In not setting deadlines with others you are creating a breeding ground for conflicts: "You promised to send it to me as soon as possible! I have been waiting for the last three days!" "I told you last Wednesday: 'as fast as possible.' Now you're bringing me the report today!"

Therefore, always make exact arrangements (*mini contracts*) in terms of deadlines! Ask or state by when a certain task must be finished, and be sure the others agree. If your ideas are incompatible with those of the others, try to find a more realistic arrangement.

13. *Priorities*	*Ranking*	*Comments*

Put down exactly what has priority over what (see Chapter 3.3).

14. *The Tyranny of the Urgent*	*Ranking*	*Comments*

Try to learn the difference between what is important and what is pressing, and refuse to be tyrannized by the urgent.

The most pressing task isn't always the most important one, but it nevertheless often takes up too much of our precious time. The tyranny of the urgent is caused if we set the wrong priorities, i.e., stress the unimportant and neglect the important things, only because a lack of planning made the unimportant things pressing.

> The important task rarely must be done today, or even this week. The urgent task calls for instant action. The momentary appeal of these tasks seems irresistible and they devour our energy. But in the light of time's perspective, their deceptive prominence fades. With a sense of loss we recall the important tasks pushed aside. We realize we've become slaves to the tyranny of the urgent.[1]

15. *Delegation*	*Ranking*	*Comments*

Right from the start you should decide which tasks you can and cannot delegate.

---

[1]Charles E. Hummel, "The Tyranny of the Urgent," in R. Alec Mackenzie. *The Time Trap* (New York: McGraw-Hill, 1975), p. 43.

| 16. *Time Wasters and Buffers* | *Ranking* | *Comments* |

An average percentage of your time should always be reserved for unexpected visitors, telephone calls, crises, or cases where you underestimated the time needed for a certain task. Try to eliminate your time wasters.

| 17. *Reviewing* | *Ranking* | *Comments* |

Regularly review whether certain activities can't be eliminated altogether.

| 18. *Free Time* | *Ranking* | *Comments* |

You should also plan or use your free time (traveling, waiting), e.g., for reading lengthy reports or conceptualizing. It would be helpful to have a time planner that contains important topics.

| 19. *Time Blocks—Uninterrupted Periods* | *Ranking* | *Comments* |

For bigger tasks, reserve longer uninterrupted periods of time as well as shorter periods for less important tasks.

| 20. *Time for Planning and Creativity* | *Ranking* | *Comments* |

You should reserve a certain amount of time for planning, preparations, creative tasks, and continuing education. If you use these periods in a different way, try to compensate for it the following week.

| 21. *Routine Tasks* | *Ranking* | *Comments* |

Routine tasks or tasks that ask for a lot of detail (e.g., monthly reports, inspections, etc.) have to be planned as well.

| 22. *Unproductive Tasks* | *Ranking* | *Comments* |

Try to keep time spent on unproductive activities (copying, unimportant meetings, etc.) to a minimum, and concentrate on the essential. Otherwise, you will be unable to use your time for more important tasks.

23. *Alternatives*	*Ranking*	*Comments*

While planning, always think of
alternatives in accord with the
following rule: "There is always
another, even better way" (Iles's law).

24. *Variety*	*Ranking*	*Comments*

Always try to have variety in your
activities to provide a balance among
long- and short-term projects,
individual tasks, and meetings.

25. *Coordinating Time Plans*	*Ranking*	*Comments*

Try to coordinate your plans with the
time plans of others (your secretary,
staff, and supervisor).

Below list the five principles you especially want to consider
within the next few weeks:

The Five Most Important Rules for My Time Planning:

1.
2.
3.
4.
5.

2.3 SYSTEM FOR TIME PLANNING

Within the overall framework of planning, time planning is
oriented toward strategic long-term goals, which can be divided into operational subobjectives. Setting time periods for
your personal and professional goals will provide you with a
feeling for and an overview of the most favorable sequence and
time allocation.

The most common periods of planning in the corporate
world are:

- Long-range = 3–5 years (or more) → Multiyear plans.
  goals

- Mid-range goals   = 1–3 years   → Yearly plans.
- Short-range goals   = 3 months–1 year   → Quarterly plans.
- Current goals = 1 week–3 months   → Monthly and weekly plans.

The following diagram depicts time planning as a closed system, in which the interrelations between the individual plans become clear: mid- and short-range as well as the current plans are derived from long-range plans, and finally lead to the planning of daily affairs. After the end of each period a debit and credit control will determine the results of each

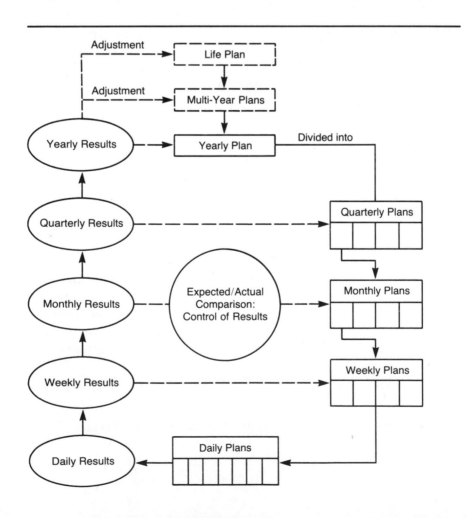

period, which (as an adjustment or correction) can be incorporated into the corresponding time plans.

Let's take a look at each of the individual plans:

1. Multiyear Plan

If you—as suggested in the preceding chapter—established a life plan of personal and professional goals, it will serve as the basis of all your planning. From the life plan you can derive your long-term goals for the next years and establish a multiyear plan.

Multiyear Plan, 1989–1994

No.	Goals (Tasks)	1989	1990	1991	1992	1993	1994
1.	Buy my own house				x	x	
2.	Become sales manager			x			
3.	Reach a yearly income of $100,000		x				

2. Yearly Plan

The next step is to derive the yearly plan from the multiyear plan. Go through the yearly columns and transfer all tasks and goals already checked. Try to see if you don't already have to tackle measures that refer to later goals.

At the year end, you should begin to determine, which tasks and goals are the most challenging for the next 12 months. A rough division into quarters will be sufficient. Since a large part of your work time will be taken up by routine work, meetings, dealings, business trips, etc., you can only budget those days that are freely at your disposal.

3. Quarterly Plans

The quarterly plan serves to control the yearly plan. We suggest that you review the past period regularly throughout the year, and, if necessary, establish contingencies for alterations and postponements. At the end of each quarter you can establish guidelines for the next three months, and determine where to cut, postpone, accelerate, or introduce new tasks.

Yearly and Quarterly Plan, 1989

		0	1	2	3	4	5	6	7	8	9	10	11	12
			I. QUARTER			II. QUARTER			III. QUARTER			IV. QUARTER		
UPDATE EDP-SYSTEM 20 DAYS	Till 11/15				×		×	×			×	×		
YEARLY REPORT 1.5 DAYS	Till 2/20			×										
STAFF EVALUATIONS 6 DAYS	Till 9/30									×	×			
SPANISH-COURSE 10 DAYS	Till 10/1								×	×	×			
MARKETING-STRATEGY '90 4 DAYS	Till 10/31										×	×		

Yearly schedule

4. Monthly Plan

You must transfer tasks and goals from the quarterly plan that have to be considered in the monthly plan. Some of these tasks and goals will also be expanded with tasks that have arisen in the meantime or have been transferred from the last monthly plan. As the duration of the plan becomes shorter, the plan

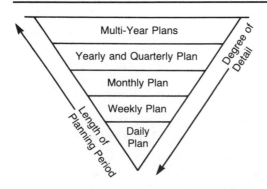

		Monthly Plan, September 89					**Activities Checklist**

D = Delegated for Action

Date	Prio-rity A|B|C|OK	Activity	Time Spent	Delegated to	D	Start Date	Due Date
	X	Update EDP system	4.0	me			9/30
Quarterly Plan	X	Staff meetings	12.0	"			9/30
	X	Intensive Spanish course	3.0	"			9/30
	X	Marketing strategy 90	3.0	"			9/30
	X	Complete market research	10.0	"		9/3	9/17
	X	Sales statistics Atlanta	8.0	Jones		9/3	9/22
	X	Talk to boss about salary	1.5	—		—	9/30
	X	Planning meeting HET	2.5	me/staff		—	9/15
	X	Prepare RKW lecture for 9/25	4.0	me		9/16	9/22

TS-form 10424 / © Copyright 1981, 87 by ▣ Time/system® International A/S . Denmark . Time/Design™ U.S. and Canada . All rights reserved.

becomes more detailed, so that an increasing number of de-tailed tasks have to be considered in the monthly plan (time invested in hours).

As a basis for realistic monthly and weekly plans you must establish your discretionary time. Try to reserve buffer time for additional and unforeseen tasks in order to keep the planned deadlines without the stress of time shortage.

5.   Weekly Plan

A weekly plan has to provide an even more detailed and pre-cise overview of the time period. Using your monthly plan as a basis, arrange all tasks and activities for the week according to scope and time. Try to follow the example on page 61:

> ### Important Questions concerning the Weekly Plan
> - What task do I have to especially concentrate on this week (main focus)?
> - What is the biggest and most time-consuming task this week?
> - What other tasks absolutely have to be finished or tack-led this week (essential tasks)?
> - What kind of routine work do I have to do (letters, tele-phone calls, meetings, etc.)?
> - What pending tasks should be tackled (optional tasks)?
> - What else would be useful, desirable, or appropriate to do?
> - What unforeseen events could be incorporated in the plan?

6.   Daily Plan

The daily plan is derived accordingly from the weekly plan. The first step is to establish which tasks and activities have to be carried out on the respective day, and new unforeseen tasks have to be added to those already planned. The daily plan is the last and most important step in time planning and the re-alization of your goals.

Period:	9/17 to 9/23 1989		**Weekly Plan**
	Offer for P-3 order		
	Marketing strategy 90		

Day	⏰	Activity	✉ ☎ OK
Mon	9 AM	Look over marketing research report + approve	1.0
	3 PM	Marketing strategy 90	1.0
	2 PM	Staff: talk to J. Biggs	1.0
		Smith: EDP trial run	✗
		Hunt + partner: marketing report	✗
Tue	11 AM	Client visiting — Moore + Co.	2.0
	9:30 AM	Meyer: insurance marketing	✗
	3 PM	Marketing strategy 90	1.0
		Minutes: planning HET meeting	✗
Wed		Offer for P-3 order	2.0
		Dr. Baines: Key-account management	✗
	9 AM	RKW lecture 9/25	2.0
	2 PM	Staff: talk to G. Warner	1.0
Thu	2 PM	Departmental meeting	1.5
	9 AM	RKW lecture 9/25	2.0
	4 PM	Marketing strategy 90	1.0
		EDP: review manual	1.0
		Martha: 25th anniversary	✗
Fri	10 AM	Talk to boss about salary	2.0
		Visit personnel office	1.0
	3 PM	Catch up on trade journals	1.0
		Newman: sales statistics Atlanta	✗
		NAM: course material	✗
Sat	11 AM	Tennis w/ George	
	8 PM	Party on Long Island	
		Aunt Bea's birthday	✗
Sun	7 PM	Dinner at in-laws'	

TS-form 1103 / © Copyright 1982, 85 by ☐ Time/system® International . Denmark . Time/Design™ U.S. and Canada . All rights reserved.

Planning calls for a step-by-step method of distributing various activities in different time periods, thus dividing the overall task into subtasks. If your work day is not effectively organized, it is probably because you did not carefully plan the allocation of your time when that time period was still in the future.

In the next section we will demonstrate the five steps of systematic planning.

2.4   TIME PLANNING (DAILY PLANS) WITH THE FIVE-STEP METHOD

Earlier we said that to plan means to prepare for achieving your goals. In terms of this we can also speak of functional plans or purposeful plans. If you have a concrete time plan, you're better able to face your environment if you know what you want, why, and when.

The most important principle is to put your plans in writing:

- You'll easily lose track of ideas and change plans that you are keeping only in your head ("Out of sight, out of mind").
- You can relieve your memory if you write down your plans.
- Writing down your plan leads psychologically to self-motivation. Your activities will be more goal-oriented, and you will follow your plan more strictly.
- You're less likely to be distracted (concentration), and you're encouraged to only deal with your desired tasks.
- In controlling daily results, unfinished tasks are not lost (you can transfer them to another day).
- On top of that, you can increase your planning success in being able to better assess your time need and disturbances and to plan for more realistic buffers for unforeseen events.

All in all, consistent time planning leads to an improvement of personal work habits.

Once you establish what you want to achieve on a certain day, you'll automatically try to organize your work so as to counteract interruptions from inside or outside. We don't waste time with unnecessary telephone calls, but if they have to be made, we should concentrate on essentials. We should question whether a planned visit is really relevant, or if the issue could also be settled with a letter or a telephone call. The reason for asking yourself at the end of a day "What have I really achieved?" often lies in the fact that a clear objective for that day was missing.[2]

A realistic daily plan should only contain what you want or must achieve—and are able to achieve! The more you think that your goals can be achieved, the more you concentrate and activate your energy to achieve that goal.

---

[2]Höhn, R. "Knowing What You Do throughout the Day—Daily Microplanning and Its Implications for Successful Management," *Economic Overview*, April 29, 1980.

The Five-Step Method

The following method is relatively simple and, with a little practice, won't take more than 10 minutes planning time each day. The five steps are:

1. Arrange your tasks.
2. Assess the length of your tasks.
3. Reserve buffers for unforeseen events (60:40 rule).
4. Decide on priorities, cuts, and delegation.
5. Review: transfer unfinished tasks.

Step 1:   Arrange Your Tasks
In the respective columns on the Daily Plan form note what you want to or have to take care of the next day:

> Planned tasks from the activities checklist or the monthly or weekly plans
> Unfinished tasks from the day before
> New tasks
> Deadlines
> Periodically recurring tasks

Use abbreviations according to the nature of the events or the respective columns on the Daily Plan form:

V — visitors
D — delegating
C — control
R — everything that has to be read (letters, memos, journals, etc.)
L — letters, mail, dictations, or everything that has to be written
P — phone calls
T — travel
S — secretary
A — activities

Here is an example of what a task list might look like:

T — BMW-dealer: used car
V — Miller (EDP list)
V — Jones (evaluation)
A — Metakom project (test market)
P — Smith (sales statistics)
L — Barnes & Co. (offer)
R — *Business Week, Barron's*
P — John (jogging)

With a little practice you can put together a task list so that you are able to:

- List the tasks tentatively according to priority.
- Divide the tasks up into labor-intensive activities and those that can be dealt with relatively quickly.
- Check whether personal communication tasks can be dealt with over the phone.

Example

A — Metakom project (test market)
V — Jones (evaluation)
T — BMW dealer (used car)
R — *Business Week, Barron's*
P — Smith (sales statistics) ⎫
L — Barnes & Co. (offer)   ⎬ Short tasks
P — Miller (EDP list)   ⎫
P — Canon (fax machine)   ⎪
P — Meyer (personnel shortage) ⎬ Telephone block
P — John (jogging)   ⎭

But this is only the beginning of your daily plan. A realistic plan should always be restricted to the tasks that can actually be tackled.

Step 2: Assess the Length of Your Tasks

Next to each task note how much time it should take, and then add up the hours:

Task	Hours
A — Metakom project (test market)	3.0
V — Jones (evaluation)	2.0
T — BMW dealer (used car)	1.5
R — *Business Week, Barron's*	1.0
P — Smith (sales statistics) } Short tasks	.5
L — Barnes & Co. (offer)	1.5
P — Miller (EDP list)	
P — Canon (fax machine) } Telephone block	.5
P — Meyer (personnel shortage)	
P — John (jogging)	
	10.0

You'll probably say that it is impossible to exactly assess how long each task will take. You're right. But with a little practice experience can serve as a basis for time planning. Your company has to make complicated assessments of future markets, sales, and costs, too.

Keep in mind that you will often need as much time for a task as is at your disposal. With a specific time frame in mind you will force yourself to keep it. If you set a certain time frame for a particular task, you will work with higher concentration and forestall interruptions with greater success. Try it for a period of 10 days, and you will see how much more confident you'll become.

Step 3: Reserve Buffers (60:40 Rule)

As a basis for your daily planning, use the 60:40 rule, which says that you shouldn't plan more than roughly 60 percent of your time. The remaining 40 percent should be reserved as a buffer for unforeseen or spontaneous events. If your workday is 10 hours long, for example, it is in your own interest not to plan for more than six hours.

However, your goal should be an eight-hour day with five planned hours! If you made plans for more than 60 percent of your available time, you will have to make rigorous cuts by setting priorities and delegating. The rest will have to be postponed, cut, or worked off in overtime.

Step 4: Decide on Priorities, Cuts, and Delegations

Your goal should be to reduce the time required for daily tasks to five or six hours. To do so, you'll need to:

Set definite priorities, e.g., with the ABC analysis, and organize your tasks (see Chapter 3).

Check your time assessment and cut it down to what is absolutely necessary; but in doing this, you must try to be realistic.

Check each activity, to see if it is possible to delegate or systematize (see the basic rules of delegation, Chapter 3.5).

You'll find further suggestions for cutting in Chapter 4.5. The final version of the daily plan in our example is as follows.

Task	Priorities	Hours	Delegated
A — Metakom project (test market)	A	2.5	.5 hr. to F.K.
V — Jones (evaluation)	A	1.5	
P — Smith (sales statistics)	B	.5	
L — Barnes & Co. (offer)	B		To H.N.
T — BMW dealer (used car)	B	1.0	
R — *Business Week, Barron's*	C		
P — Miller (EDP list)	C		
P — Canon (fax machine)	C	0.5	To secretary
P — Meyer (personnel shortage)	C		
P — John (jogging)	C		
		6.0	

The completed Daily Plan form is shown on page 68:

NOVEMBER	DECEMBER	JANUARY	**Daily Plan**	**Wednesday**

NOVEMBER
S M T W T F S
1 2 3 4
5 6 7 8 9 10 11
12 13 14 15 16 17 18
19 20 21 22 23 24 25
26 27 28 29 30

DECEMBER
S M T W T F S
1 2
3 4 5 6 7 8 9
10 11 12 13 14 15 16
17 18 19 20 21 22 23
24 25 26 27 28 29 30
31

JANUARY
S M T W T F S
1 2 3 4 5 6
7 8 9 10 11 12 13
14 15 16 17 18 19 20
21 22 23 24 25 26 27
28 29 30 31

Daily Plan   **Wednesday**

13

Week 50   349/17   **December 1989**

🕐	Schedule	OK	✉ ☎ Contact	OK
			Miller (EDP list)	
			Canon (fax machine)	
8:00	Quiet hour		Meyer (personnel shortage)	
9:			John (jogging)	
10:			Tip from Susan Hill	
11:00	Telephone block		781-2328	
12:00	BMW			
1:				
2:00	Talk w/Jones (evaluation)			
3:				

#	Activity	
A	MetaKom project	2.5
A	Jones (evaluation)	1.5
B	Smith (sales statistics)	0.5
B	BMW dealer	1.0
C	Business Week, Barrons	.5
Del.	MetaKom project >F.K.	0.5
Del.	Barnes + Co. (offer) >H.N.	1.5

4:	Smith—sales statistics
5:00	Daily plan 12/15
6:	
7:	
8:	
9:	
10:	

Statistics   AM   PM
Interruptions   ₦₦ /   //

Daily goal—
Successful from now on!

Personal
Flowers for Hillary

TS-form 11350 / © Copyright 1982, 87 by ⊡ Time/system® International A/S. Denmark. Time/Design™ U.S. and Canada. All rights reserved.

Step 5:   Review : Transfer of Unfinished Tasks
Experience shows that you can't finish all activities or make all phone calls as planned. They'll have to be transferred to the next day. After you've transferred an activity many times, it will start to bother you. There are two possibilities:

You will finally tackle the activity and finish it once and for all.

You can just cut it from the list because the matter has been settled by itself.

Since conventional appointment books do not supply enough space for daily plans, you will soon lose control and end up with a system of loose pages. Therefore, it is advisable to work regularly and consistently with a time planner. There you'll find daily plans, time plans, and other systematized plans (see the examples in Chapter 2.5).

Systematizing through *Bureauglyphics*

When filling in forms you can further systematize your entries by using not only letter abbreviations but other abbreviations and graphic symbols as well, which we'll refer to as *bureauglyphics*. Here are some examples:

x urgent

! important

? clarify

↘ A priorities

• a completed task

•• a very well completed task

○ transfer task to a later time

× a nonfeasible task or a matter that has taken care of itself

You can also make up your own symbols. There is no limit to your creativity. Through the use of abbreviations and signs you can increase the effectiveness of your time planner even more.

Summary: What the Five-Step Method Can Do for You

If you work with the five-step method for 20 minutes each night (later you'll only need five or 10 minutes), you will recoup this time many times over. Here again are the most important reasons for the five-step method:

Twenty Advantages of the Five-Step Method

You're better attuned to the next workday.

You can plan the next day.

You have a clear overview of the demands of the day.

Your whole day is organized.

You avoid forgetting things you have to do.

You can concentrate on what's important.

You avoid dissipating your energies.

You can attain your daily goals.

You can distinguish between important and less important activities.

You can decide on priorities and matters to be delegated.

You systematize by grouping tasks together.

You decrease disturbances and interruptions and handle them better.

You are more disciplined in dealing with your tasks.

You can decrease stress.

You can keep calm when faced with unforeseen events.

You improve your self-control.

You feel the positive effect of success at the end of the day.

Your satisfaction and motivation are increased.

You can increase your productivity.

And most of all you can save time through systematic work habits.

Let's mention the last and most important aspect once again: by successfully applying time-planning techniques and work habits, you can save between 10 and 20 percent of your time every day! In this way you can gain one hour a day: the *GOLDEN HOUR.*

Try to plan your workday with the five-step method for a month. Even though you'll need a little self-discipline, you will soon see the great advantages of daily time planning.

When Do You Start? Tomorrow?   Date: _____

Make your plans before you start working—as early as the evening before the next workday. You'll go home feeling more confident and relaxed, and the next morning you're going to start the day with much higher concentration!

The Psychological Background

On your ride to and from the office, you can begin to subconsciously deal with tasks and prepare possible solutions.

Since you have the main tasks and possible solutions already in mind, the new, busy day won't seem like a big burden anymore; it will become clearer, easier to plan and grasp.

You'll be much less prone to be sidetracked by irrelevant matters, which used to be such a good reason for putting off main tasks more and more until you could only deal with them (less satisfactorily) under time pressure by means of overtime.

What to Do Next?

1. In addition to the detailed daily plan, all of us should at least make a rough yearly plan.
2. Next, you can add weekly and then monthly plans.
3. Integrated, complete time planning includes a quarterly plan; at last all levels of the system—from the yearly to the daily plan—are covered (See diagram on p. 56).
4. If your professional or personal goals allow it, you can even expand the system into a multiperiod plan or a life plan.

For daily planning we recommend using what is probably the most effective means—the time planner or time-planning book.

2.5   MANAGEMENT WITH A TIME PLANNER

The Perils of Conventional Appointment Books.   You probably have already tried to plan your day before—but not as consciously, methodically, and systematically as shown in this chapter. You probably have kept an appointment book, most likely in the form of a pocket calendar or a big, more or less decorative desk calendar.

Conventional appointment calendars that can only be used to note appointments are the grave diggers of successful time planning. The value of such notebooks normally is in helping you to remember deadlines and dates that, like a train schedule, determine the stops—or various phases—of your workday. But these notebooks fail to note what really has to be achieved. That is because each of our activities has a goal—something we want to or must achieve. The expression "what has to be done" describes simply the content of my tasks. But when I speak about "what I want to achieve," then I am clearly directing my activities toward my goals.

If we take a closer look at conventional appointment books, we can come up with the following critique of them:

10 Flaws of Appointment Books
1. A schedule is given only for deadlines and dates, not for the goals of activities. What is really important isn't noted in the daily plan.
2. The length of activities isn't given; buffer times are not supplied for longer activities.
3. The activities are listed in an arbitrary way, influenced by external factors.
4. There is no daily planning—no thinking ahead.
5. There is no mention of blocks of time for work and buffer times for unforeseen tasks (e.g., 90 minutes of planned work and 30 minutes of buffer time).

6. Routine meetings are listed without naming the topic.
7. Activities aren't listed according to priorities.
8. Activities are not clearly defined (e.g., a meeting with the boss).
9. There is no time planned for routine or permanent work.
10. No checklists or other forms are provided to help in planning.

Conclusion: I need to use a time planner.

What Is a Time Planner?   It is a system of loose pages held together in a binder, clearly and systematically divided into sections. It is an appointment book, diary, notebook, planning instrument, memory help, address book, encyclopedia, catalogue of ideas, and control instrument all in one. It is your personal and constant companion—your written memory always at hand. We recommend a $6'' \times 9''$ format, as smaller binders do not provide enough space for all the entries and forms, and won't give you enough of an overview. The time planner is the practical part of a consistent time-planning system, containing all time plans, forms, and lists for daily use.

What Should a Time Planner Look Like?   Depending on the manufacturer, a time planner might consist of the following parts.

Calendar Part.   Besides a folding yearly calendar you might also want to have the various forms for monthly, weekly, and daily plans as well as an index. The daily plan is especially important. Its main principle is one page per day. A page marker might be useful here, as it allows you to quickly find a particular day. There should be pages for noting appointments for the following weeks and months from which you can transfer your notes easily. After using the daily sheets you can periodically file them into separate binders for further reference. Deadlines and tasks can be transferred from the weekly or monthly sheets to newly added daily sheets; the same can be done for dates for birthdays, anniversaries, vacations, events, payments, etc. from their respective lists. This way you can integrate all private matters, and nothing will get lost.

Professional and Personal Data.   Here you can always carry the most important lists and information in compact form on a set of forms with you, e.g., the following:

Project management items
Dates for fairs/exhibits and seminars
Miniorganizational plans
Important function abbreviations
Wage rates/salary scales
Turnover tables
List of birthdays
Mailing rates
Booklists
Airplane schedules
Hotel addresses
Travel expenses
Caloric tables
Dates of events
Notes
Blank sheets
Universal planning sheets
Ideas catalogue
Checklists

Address and Telephone Directories.   You'll always have the most important telephone numbers and addresses at hand.

Miscellaneous.   Separate compartments in the time planner should provide room for additional items, such as checks, stamps, credit cards, IDs, passport photos, or money.

Putting into Practice
With a time planner you'll be able to better plan, organize, co-ordinate your (weekly, monthly) work, and use your time more

efficiently. A time planner increases the quality and success of your work. If you systematize your time with it only 12.5 percent, you'll save one hour in an eight-hour day. Therefore, carry a time planner—it is the most important means of self-management!

2.6 SUMMARY AND ANALYSIS

Planning in terms of self-management means getting ready to realize goals. With a little more time spent for planning you can decrease the actual time needed to implement your tasks and ultimately even save time (planning = time saving). The benefits of planning self-management and time management are that you can reach your goals, save time, maintain an overview, set priorities, set deadlines, keep time reserves (buffers); you'll be more efficient; you can delegate more; and you'll reduce stress (see the checklist in Chapter 2.1).

The most important principles and rules of time planning are:

1. The 60:40 rule
2. Analysis of activities and time/interruptions
3. List of tasks/activities
4. Regularity and consistency
5. Planning realistically
6. Flexibility
7. Time losses
8. Putting it into writing
9. Unaccomplished tasks
10. Results—not activities
11. Time frames
12. Deadlines
13. Priorities
14. The tyranny of the urgent
15. Delegation
16. Time wasters and buffers
17. Reviewing
18. Free time

19. Blocks of time and uninterrupted periods
20. Time for planning and creativity
21. Routine tasks
22. Unproductive tasks
23. Alternatives
24. Variety
25. Coordinating time plans

Time planning can be depicted as a closed system: weekly and monthly plans are derived from quarterly and yearly plans as well as from multiyear plans and life plans. After a comparison between the target date for completing a task and the actual date, you can make adjustments. (You can compare the time-planning system with a set of building blocks.) The plan is the last and most important step in time planning; it is the realization of your goals. Planning calls for a step-by-step method of distributing various tasks in different time periods, thus dividing the overall tasks into subtasks (from the action plan to the time plan).

In investing 10 to 20 minutes per day in the five-step-method you can save time. The five steps tell you to:

1. List all tasks.
2. Assess the length of tasks.
3. Reserve buffers (60:40 rule).
4. Decide on priorities, cuts, and delegation.
5. Review and transfer unfinished tasks to a later target date.

A time planner is the most important and effective means of personal self-management. It is a calendar, diary, note book, catalogue of ideas, and means of control—all in one.

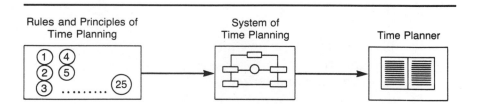

Rules and Principles of Time Planning   System of Time Planning   Time Planner

At the beginning it is important to establish a global yearly plan and to work with daily plans. You should have a positive attitude towards the plan—it is a step toward achieving your goals.

Even a busy manager is free to change specific goals and plans in such a way as to accommodate his or her life plan or career plan. Try it! You need to stay alert and flexible so that you can react to all kinds of influences—for example, to things or events that may interfere with your objectives. A sound plan will help you remain calm.

Constantly review and rearrange your plans if they can't be carried out, or if the date set for a particular goal cannot be accomplished. But once you decide on a certain goal, go through with it and concentrate all your energy on it. But keep in mind that tension has to be followed by relaxation: managing your health is a part of self-management. Above all, don't concentrate on material or professional success alone!

Now make your own analysis of this chapter and ask yourself the following questions:

- What seemed of special importance to me?
- What new insights did I gain?
- Were any of my assumptions confirmed?
- Which suggestions do I want to put into practice?

Analysis of Chapter 2

Result No.	Pages	Ideas, Suggestions, Topics of Value	Target Dates for Attainment	Control

So when you have to deal with the goals, means, ways, and time connected with your professional and personal life, remember to work with plans!

CHAPTER 3

DECISION MAKING: HOW TO INVOKE HIDDEN ENERGIES AND FREE UP YOUR TIME

Efficiency may be defined as doing any job right . . .
Effectiveness as doing the **right** job right.

Peter Drucker

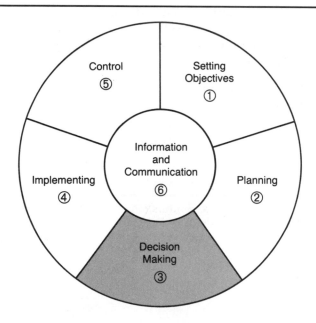

This chapter deals with the criteria and methods necessary to find the "right" tasks for a successful work technique.

3.1 THE IMPORTANCE OF DECISION MAKING

In terms of self-management, decision making refers to selecting those tasks that have priority on the basis of their nature and scope. Decision making means to set priorities. Two of the major problems of managers are that they often want to deal with too many tasks and they lose themselves in often unimportant, but seemingly necessary tasks.

At the end of a day of hard work, you will probably realize that you have worked a lot, but left many important matters unfinished. Many managers justify this unsatisfactory situation by saying, "There are just so many important tasks each day!" Successful managers distinguish themselves by dealing not only with many tasks but also with a wide variety of tasks, and by concentrating on just one task at a time. They finish only one task at a time, but they do it with resolve and with a goal in mind. This requires setting priorities even—or especially—for the most important tasks, establishing a priority list and adhering to it.

To illustrate this simple, basic, but often overlooked correlation, here's the well-known anecdote of the $25,000 piece of advice:

> When Charles M. Schwab was president of Bethlehem Steel, he confronted Ivy Lee, a management consultant, with an unusual task: "Show me a way to better use my time", he said. "If it works, I'll pay you any fee within reasonable limits." Lee handed Schwab a sheet of paper and said: "Write down the most important things you'll have to do tomorrow, and number them according to their significance. Tomorrow morning you'll start with task no. 1 and stay with it, until it is finished. Check your priorities again, and then start with no. 2, and don't go on until you've finished this one. Then you'll proceed to no. 3 and so on. . . . Even if you can't keep your time plan, it's not that bad. By the end of the day you'll have finished the most important tasks, before tasks of less importance take up your time. The secret is to do it daily: check the relative importance of the tasks you'll

have to deal with, decide over priorities, list them in a daily plan and stick to it. Make it your habit for every work day. When you're convinced of the value of the system, pass it on to your staff. Try it for as long as you like and then send me a check for as much as you think the advice is worth."

A couple of weeks later Schwab sent Lee a check for $25,000. Later Schwab said that this had been the most profitable lesson he ever learned in his management career[1]

Setting priorities means to decide which task comes first, second, etc., or which can be dealt with later.

Setting priorities seems so obvious, it is often done unsystematically and even unconsciously. Therefore set clear priorities consciously and finish your planned tasks with resolve and in order.

The benefits of setting priorities are that you'll:

Work only on important or necessary tasks.

Also work on urgent tasks if necessary.

Focus on one task at a time.

Purposefully tackle and finish tasks within a given time period.

Best reach your goals under the circumstances.

Eliminate all tasks that can be carried out by someone else.

Finish the most important tasks by the end of a planning period (e.g., a workday).

Not leave unfinished tasks vital in assessing you and your productivity.

The positive effects are that you'll:

Keep deadlines.

Do your work more easily and attain better results.

Be on better terms with your staff, colleagues, and superiors.

---

[1]R. A. Mackenzie, *The Time Trap* (New York: McGraw-Hill, 1975), pp. 38–39.

Avoid conflicts.

Become more satisfied and avoid unnecessary stress.

The following sections will introduce a variety of criteria and methods for you to use in deciding how to sequence your most important tasks.

3.2   THE PARETO TIME PRINCIPLE (80:20 RULE)

The Pareto principle generally implies that within a given group or quantity some parts are of much higher value than their relative share in the total would suggest. Named after the Italian economist Vilfredo Pareto (1848–1923), it has been proven valid in many areas. For example, two American technicians applying the Pareto principle to inventory control discovered that 20 percent of the stock made up 80 percent of the value of the inventory. Concentrating controls on these essential few elements brought net results that far exceeded in effectiveness all previous inventory work.

Other examples from the business world show that:

20 percent of the clients (or products) generate 80 percent of the sales or profit.

80 percent of the clients (or products) generate 20 percent of the sales or profit.

20 percent of the mistakes cause 80 percent of the rejects.

80 percent of the mistakes cause 20 percent of the rejects.

20 percent of the products make up 80 percent of the production costs.

80 percent of the products make up 20 percent of the production costs.

Therefore, the Pareto principle is also known as the "80:20 rule." Applying this rule to the work situation of a manager means that: In the productivity process the first 20 percent of the time spent (input) achieves 80 percent of the productivity results (output). The remaining 80 percent of the time spent only accounts for 20 percent of the total results.

The following diagram shows this rule of thumb of time management:

Pareto Time Principle (80:20 Rule)

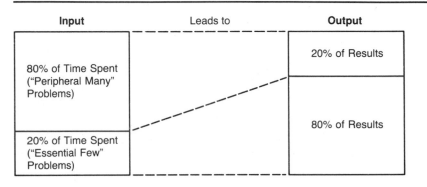

For your daily work it means that you should proceed according to priority—not turn to the easiest, most interesting tasks or to tasks that take the least amount of time. Tackle the essential few problems before the peripheral many! The Pareto time principle can be practically applied in analyzing all tasks in terms of their share of end results, dividing them into categories A, B, and C (as explained below).

3.3   SETTING PRIORITIES THROUGH THE ABC ANALYSIS

The ABC analysis is based on the principle that the percentage distribution of very important and somewhat less important tasks generally remains constant. The letters A, B, and C divide the various tasks into three groups according to their significance in achieving professional and personal goals. Numerous managers use the principle of first tackling the most important tasks of their daily work first.

Use the ABC analysis to complete this personal exercise in systematic planning and to improve your work habits. Plan your time according to the importance and value of tasks and not their percentage of the total of all tasks.

The ABC analysis is based on the following three facts:

1. The most important tasks (A tasks) make up 15 percent of all managerial tasks and activities. The actual value of these tasks (in terms of their contribution to goal achievement) is 65 percent.
2. Tasks of average importance (B tasks) make up about 20 percent of the total and 20 percent of the value of managerial tasks and activities.
3. Less important or unimportant tasks (C tasks), however, make up 65 percent of the total of all tasks, but only 15 percent of the value of all managerial tasks.

ABC Analysis

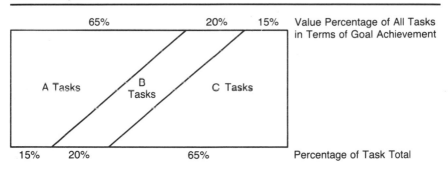

It is advisable to use the ABC analysis to tackle the most important, i.e., the most productive tasks first (A tasks) in order to achieve the greatest amount of the success from the fewest activities. The second most important tasks (B tasks) achieve a certain increase in rewards, whereas the relatively high number of less important tasks (C tasks) only make a small contribution. The following graph illustrates this evaluation:

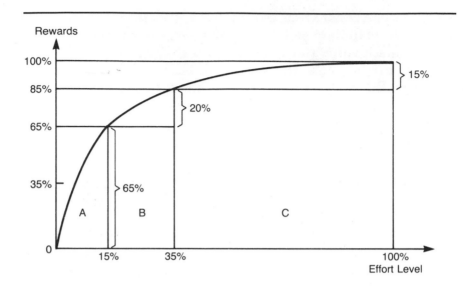

In using the ABC analysis for your tasks, you can do the following:

1. List all the planned tasks for the time period in question (week, day, etc.). See the category entitled *tasks* in your daily plan (discussed earlier) or use the Activities Checklist.
2. Arrange the tasks according to their importance, i.e., to their significance for your goal.
3. Number the tasks (see the time planning forms in Chapter 2).
4. Evaluate your tasks according to the ABC framework:
   A. The first 15 percent of all tasks are A tasks (very important, of great value for goal achievement, can't be delegated).
   B. The next 20 percent of all tasks are B tasks (important, significant, can be delegated).
   C. The remaining 65 percent of all tasks are C tasks (less important, insignificant, can be delegated in any case).
5. Starting with the A tasks, check if the time budgeted in your time plan corresponds with the significance of tasks:

65 percent of available time (= about three hours) for A tasks.
20 percent of available time (= about one hour) for B tasks.
15 percent of available time (= about 45 minutes) for C tasks.

6. If necessary, make adjustments. In aligning your time plan with your A tasks, you automatically ensure that the less important, but time-consuming C tasks get assigned only as much time as is concomitant with their significance.
7. Check if B and C tasks can be delegated (see Chapter 3.5). Keep in mind though, that not all C tasks are dispensable. In addition to the A and B tasks, you must do some amount of routine work as well.

Organizing your tasks with the help of the ABC analysis can be done, as the form shown below indicates. (You might want to add this form to your time planner.)

Activities Checklist

Activities Checklist

D = Delegated for Action

Date	Prio-rity A	B	C	OK	Activity	Delegated to	D	Start Date	Due Date

Source: Time/system® and Time/Design® are registered trademarks belonging to Time/system as, Denmark.

Deciding priorities—like the business of setting goals—is a very individual process, since every situation analysis is ultimately subjective. Priorities are debatable, and objective results very unlikely. What's important is the fact that you're setting clear priorities and basing your decision on facts as much as possible. Self-management requires you as manager (to a large degree) to decide which tasks have to be done and in what chronological order.

Criteria for A Tasks.   The following questions are designed to help you setting priorities and determining A tasks:

What tasks are instrumental in coming closer to my main goals (yearly, monthly, weekly, and daily goals)?

Is it possible to cover several problems in executing just one task?

By executing what task can I contribute the most toward achieving the goals of the organization, department, or work group?

By executing what task do I gain the most, get rewarded the most, and gain the highest recognition?

Which task presents the greatest risk of strong negative reactions (trouble, criticism, or disturbance) if I don't get to it?

Setting Priorities Is the Basis of a Successful Work Technique.   You have to realize that you can't and needn't do everything. Set priorities and start with what is most important!

3.4   A QUICK ANALYSIS ACCORDING TO THE EISENHOWER PRINCIPLE

Very often our energy is used up in matters that are pressing, i.e., have a very short deadline but are really not that important. Thus the saying: "Important matters are never pressing, and pressing matters are seldom important." An important task very rarely has to be carried out today or this week, but a pressing task has to be carried out immediately. Ask yourself:

> Do I tend to hurry from one pressing task to another?
>
> Is this why really important tasks are often left undone?

A principle attributed to General Dwight D. Eisenhower will help you to quickly decide which tasks should have priority. You have to set priorities according to the criteria of immediacy and importance.

You can differentiate among four possible ways of evaluating and executing tasks according to the degree of their immediacy and importance:

The Eisenhower Principle

More Important	**B Tasks** (Terminate or delegate)	**A Tasks** (To deal with right away)
Less Important	W	**C Tasks** (To delegate)
	Less Immediate	More Immediate

Immediate/Important Tasks. You have to deal with these right away.

Immediate/Less Important Tasks. Here you run the risk of being overcome by the "tyranny of the urgent" and of dealing with the problem yourself—because it so immediate. If this task is of lesser importance, however, you should delegate it since it will not be very demanding.

Less Immediate/Important Tasks. They can wait because they don't have to be dealt with immediately. This will be the rule in most cases. These tasks will become problematic, though, if sooner or later they become immediate and you have to deal with them yourself.

Suggestion: Try to delegate these tasks in part or altogether to your staff. Besides you getting relieved of work, your staff will be better motivated and become better prepared to deal with demanding tasks. (There will be more on delegation in the next section of this chapter.)

Less Immediate/Less Important Tasks. Very often tasks of this category get dumped onto a desk that is already piled high. Once you start dealing with such tasks and therefore neglecting tasks in category no. I, don't be surprised if you're overworked. You shouldn't even use your staff for tasks of this kind.

Refrain from tasks that are of less immediacy and less importance. Have the courage to take a risk and decide more often in favor of filing them in the wastebasket. Your productivity will increase significantly if you consistently categorize your work according to the Eisenhower principle. Here again are its most important advantages:

You start with and concentrate exclusively on the most important tasks.

You free up your time for key managerial tasks, such as motivating your staff.

You make your staff share responsibility, and you don't just delegate to them less important or routine work.

You can challenge and promote high-quality employees.

3.5 UNDERSTANDING DELEGATION

In general, *delegation* means transferring tasks and activities from the desk of the manager to that of a subordinate. The authority needed for the task and the responsibility for the means to achieve it should be delegated along with the task itself. Leadership responsibility remains with the superior—it can't be delegated.

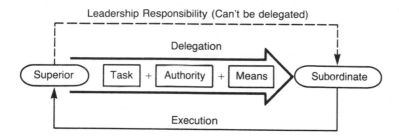

A task or activity can be delegated:

- Permanently (permanent or general delegation); this means that the manager hands over a task to a subordinate, who has to take care of it on his or her own.
- Only for specific cases (ad hoc delegation); this means that the task stays within the superior's functional area.

Delegation is the key activity of every manager. Its direct and indirect benefits are significant.

1. Benefits of Delegation

Check the following arguments on the benefits of delegation you agree with:

- Delegation makes things easier for managers and helps them gain time for important tasks (e.g., for true leadership).
- Delegation capitalizes on the knowledge and experience of subordinates.
- Delegation helps to further and develop the abilities, initiative, independence, and competencies of subordinates.
- Delegation often has a positive effect on the motivation and job satisfaction of subordinates.

Did you check several or even all of these points? If so, you'll have to agree that delegation has benefits for both managers and subordinates. Subordinates generally react positively to delegation. A study in which 500 groups of managers were evaluated by their staff showed that managers who often delegated were evaluated as very good or good, whereas managers who delegated ineffectively received poor evaluations.

Given the above-mentioned benefits, why is delegation still so uncommon? One reason for inadequate delegation is personal, e.g., some people feel an aversion to delegation in general; another reason is the bad way in which the act of delegating is handled. Successful delegating therefore requires two things: (1) the *willingness* to delegate; and (2) the *ability* to delegate.

If you have problems with willingness, analyze your or your subordinates' resistance to the idea. (We'll take up this problem in the next section.) If you have problems with ability, you should keep the principles of delegation in mind. (We discuss them in pages 88–89 of this chapter.)

2. Resistance to Delegation

Very few managers handle delegation perfectly. Many delegate reluctantly or insufficiently. It isn't necessary to become a perfectionist where delegation is concerned—but try to find out where you can improve your delegating style. Here is a list of reasons why delegation might be resisted. Consider which of these might apply to your situation:

- Since you have a very demanding work situation (visitors, telephone calls, meetings, and deadlines), there is no time left for explaining or monitoring tasks that are to be delegated.
- Maybe you don't know enough about the task and the problems involved, so it's unclear to you exactly what to delegate to your staff.
- You decide against delegating because you think you can finish the task faster than anyone on your staff and save time.
- You're afraid of a conflict with your superior if you delegate a task entrusted to you.
- You're attached to a certain task or activity which is fun to do.

- You're afraid your staff will deal better with the task than you could, that is, you fear competition.
- You're afraid of losing control, once the task is out of your hands.
- You don't have confidence in the ability of your subordinates, and you don't want to run the risk.
- You're afraid to lose authority or prestige if tasks formerly taken care of by you are taken care of by your staff.
- You don't know how to react if a subordinate rejects a task.

How can you overcome your personal resistance to delegation? List some ideas or strategies.

-
-
-
-
-

Subordinates can also resist delegation.

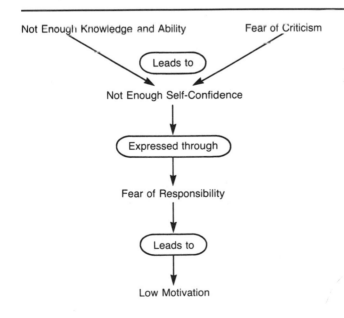

If you have the feeling that a subordinate resists delegation of tasks, talk to him or her openly and directly. Try to find
out the reasons for this resistance and develop with that person
possible solutions (e.g., supportive measures or support from
you as the superior). Keep in mind, though, that your style of
delegation might be the problem. Inadequate delegation techniques can lead to frustration and resistance on the part of the
staff, which might reflect back on you as the manager and over
time create an outright fear of delegation. But there is no
effective management without effective delegation!

3. How Well Do You Delegate?

In listing your activities and making an ABC analysis, you will
detect a number of B and especially C tasks that you can or
should delegate. Delegation always means taking some of the
burden off your shoulders and saving time for really important
tasks (A tasks). How do you know how well you deal with delegation? When you don't delegate enough, doesn't that cause a
major problem? The following questions can give you some
information:

How Well Do You Delegate?

Questions to Ask Yourself	Yes/No
1. Do I work long after office hours? Do I take home work on a regular basis?	_____
2. Do I work longer than my staff?	_____
3. Do I spend time doing things for other people that they could do themselves?	_____
4. In an emergency, is there no subordinate or colleague who could relieve me?	_____
5. Do any of my colleagues, subordinates (or my boss) know my work well enough to take over if I had to leave it?	_____
6. Do I lack the time to plan my tasks and activities?	_____
7. When I return from a business trip is my desk piled high?	_____
8. Do I still deal with activities or problems that were my responsibility before I got promoted?	_____
9. Do I often have to postpone an important task to deal with others?	_____
10. Am I constantly in a hurry in order to meet deadlines?	_____
11. Do I spend time with routine work that could be done by someone else?	_____

Questions to Ask Yourself	Yes/No
12. Do I dictate most of the correspondence, memos, and reports that I have to sign?	_____
13. Do staff members often approach me with questions concerning meetings, projects, or tasks?	_____
14. Do I lack time for social or company functions?	_____
15. Do I want to be involved in and informed about everything?	_____
16. Do I have a hard time following my priority list?	_____

Add up how many times you answered with yes:

! 0–3 yeses: You delegate extraordinarily well! You can skip the rest of the chapter.

? 4–7 yeses: You could improve your delegation style in several areas.

↯ 8 or more yeses: You have a serious problem with delegation. Solving this problem should have absolute priority for you!

3.6 THE BASIC RULES OF DELEGATION

As a manager you have certain duties when it comes to delegation:

Choosing the right staff member.

Defining and monitoring areas of responsibility.

Coordinating delegated tasks.

Supporting and giving advice to staff members.

Informing staff members sufficiently and in a timely fashion.

Controlling processes and outcomes.

Evaluating staff members (praise often, but give constructive criticism, too).

Trying to fend off attempts to return a task or delegate it further.

The staff members have duties as well when it comes to executing delegated tasks:

Acting independently and autonomously within the frame of delegation.

Admitting to improper actions or decisions.

Informing the superior in time of problems.

Presenting exceptional cases to the superior (Management by Exception).

Discussing and coordinating activities with other staff members.

Continuing their education in order to meet job demands if necessary.

The manager's problem is not how much he or she *should* delegate to relieve stress and save time but rather how much he or she *can* delegate without asking too much of the staff. The higher your standing as a manager is in the hierarchy, the more time you should spend on real management tasks, and the less time you will have for routine tasks.

What Can You Delegate—and What Can You Not Delegate?
You can always delegate:

- Routine work
- Tasks requiring special knowledge
- Details
- Preparations (such as designs)

All the same, in some instances you'll need to analyze each task to determine how feasible it is to delegate it. For example, you may let a subordinate draft—but not finalize—goals, plans, programs, or projects on which you'll have to decide later. Or at a meeting you may have a staff member present an analysis of certain problems as well as suggestions for solving them. You might also delegate some middle- or long-term tasks to a staff member in order to motivate or professionally advance that individual.

You *can't* delegate:

- Real leadership activities, e.g., setting goals, decisions on company politics, monitoring results, and so forth
- The task of leading and motivating your staff
- Tasks with far-reaching implications or consequences
- High-risk tasks
- Exceptional cases
- Critical, pressing tasks when there is no time for explanations and control
- Confidential matters

Which tasks do I already delegate to my staff?

-
-
-
-
-

Which tasks can I and do I want to delegate in the future?

-
-
-
-
-

When Do You Delegate?

In your daily work situation, you should delegate as much and as often as is possible. If there are basic changes in your situation, you should delegate in order to redistribute tasks and responsibilities. Such changes might include (1) staff changes (new hires, promotions, or departures); (2) reorganizing and re-structuring of your department; (3) special events and crises; and (4) the addition of new areas of responsibility.

To Whom Do You Delegate?

In principle you should delegate only to staff members directly subordinate to you. Don't delegate only to the most capable (and busiest) staff members who can take on additional work or to staff members who have free time at their disposal. Instead, you should take into consideration staff members who want to take on difficult tasks, who need more experience, and whose abilities need to be tested and developed.

Also, think about other departments as well as external service groups if your objective is to get rid of unnecessary work.

Tasks and Activities	Departments and Service Groups

How Do You Delegate?
Here are 20 rules that should result in successful delegation:

1. Delegate as early as possible. Make decisions on what you want or have to delegate right after you make your work plan.
2. Delegate according to the abilities and capacities of your staff members.
3. Delegate in terms of your staff member's motivation and development.
4. If possible, delegate complete tasks, and not only isolated subtasks.
5. Make clear whether the delegation is ad hoc or permanent.
6. If possible, delegate similar tasks permanently to a certain staff member.
7. Make sure that the respective staff member is able to and wants to take on the task.
8. Resist the temptation to give the same task to two staff members to ensure it gets done.

9. Together with the task, delegate the necessary authority and general responsibility.
10. Inform and instruct the staff member as precisely and completely as possible about his or her task, and make sure that everything is understood. (The staff member can act only according to what you told him or her, not according to what you have in mind.)
11. Explain the aim and object of the task (motivation and goal setting).
12. Delegate extensive and important tasks in writing if necessary.
13. Use the following five-step method if faced with new and complicated tasks.
    A. Prepare your staff member.
    B. Explain the task.
    C. Demonstrate the work.
    D. Let the staff member imitate your work and then correct him or her.
    E. Leave the job with the staff member and then check on what he or she does.
14. If necessary, give the staff member the possibility to expand his or her knowledge on a demanding task.
15. Facilitate your staff member's access to the necessary information.
16. Strictly avoid unnecessary interference in the performance of the task, thus thwarting the delegation.
17. Give the impression, though, that the staff member can come to you for advice and support if he or she faces difficulties and problems.
18. Ask for progress reports at designated intervals.
19. Monitor the task results and immediately inform the staff member of your evaluation.
20. Praise successful aspects and give constructive criticism of shortcomings and failures. If necessary, let the staff member identify the task as his or hers for superiors or let the staff member take part in presentations in front of committees.

The Six W Rules of Delegation.   You can use the following six W rules as a checklist for delegation:

WHAT?
What is there to do in general?
What individual tasks are to be dealt with?
What results are we striving for?
What deviations from this norm are acceptable?
What difficulties are to be expected?

WHO?
Who is the most capable for this task or activity?
Who should assist in carrying it out?

WHY?
What is the purpose and goal of the activity or task?
What happens if the task is not carried out or carried out incompletely?

IN WHAT WAY?
In what way should the implementation be carried out?
Which procedures will be applied?
What regulations have to be observed?
Which departments have to be informed?
What could the costs be?

WITH WHAT?
What means have to be applied?
What equipment does the staff member need?
What documents are needed?

WHEN?
When does the work have to start?
When does the work have to be finished?
What interim deadlines have to be kept?
When do I want to be informed about the progress of the task?
When do I have to monitor the task, in order to be able to intervene, if necessary?

Monitoring Delegated Tasks.   Make a list of the delegations for which you are responsible so that you can stay in control of all delegated tasks and deadlines. Here is an example of such a list.

Project Management				
Title				
Ref.				
Date Dept.			Page	

Task				OK
Goal/Purpose				

Major components				
1				
2				
3				
4				
5				
6				
7				
8				
9				
10				

Action steps	Dele-gated to	Comple-tion Time	Follow-up	Due Date
1				
2				
3				
4				
5				
6				
7				
8				
9				
10				
11				
12				
13				
14				
15				
16				
17				

3.7   SUMMARY AND ANALYSIS

To work successfully means doing the right things accurately and well. Making decisions in terms of self-management means setting goal-oriented, clear priorities. A personal priority list is absolutely necessary if you intend to carry out your tasks effectively.

Establishing and setting priorities helps you to:

Finish tasks according to plan.

Finish pressing tasks on schedule.

Control disruptions.

Find alternatives.

Consider the possibilities of delegation.

Establishing and setting priorities enables you to:

Actively control the work process (self-management).

Avoid unnecessary conflicts of goals.

Avoid conflicts with your staff, colleagues, and superiors.

Avoid double work.

Avoid unnecessary stress.

The Pareto time principle (80:20 rule) is an effective way to organize your time. If you consider all tasks in terms of effectiveness, 80 percent of all effective results are achieved in only 20 percent of the time spent, whereas the remaining 20 percent of results are achieved in 80 percent of the time. Therefore, the essential few problems should be dealt with before the peripheral many.

The ABC analysis ensures that your tasks are organized according to the correct priority and that results are monitored in terms of goal achievement, as shown in the following table.

A Tasks	B Tasks	C Tasks
Extremely important	Of average importance	Less important, or unimportant
Make up 15% of all tasks and 65% of their value	Make up 20% of all tasks and 20% of their value	Make up 65% of all tasks and 15% of their value
Do yourself, and do not delegate	Try to delegate in part	Delegate, shorten, or cut out

- You have to realize that you can't do everything; set your priorities and start with the most important tasks (basic rule of successful work method).
- An important task rarely has to be finished today or this week, whereas pressing tasks have to be dealt with immediately.
- Free yourself of the tyranny of the urgent; you should never let important tasks become pressing, and you should try to delegate pressing, but less important tasks to others.
- Use the Eisenhower principle consistently, and don't be afraid to throw less pressing or less important tasks into the wastebasket.
- Delegation means transferring tasks and authority plus responsibility.
- Delegation means taking some of the work load off yourself, creating time for leadership tasks (A tasks), and giving staff members a chance to develop (motivation).
- Delegation is equally beneficial for both manager and staff members.
- Delegation requires the willingness and the ability to delegate.
- Noneffective delegation means noneffective management.

- Delegate supervised middle- and long-term tasks, too, in order to motivate your staff members.
- Delegate daily as much and as often as possible to the extent that the circumstances and capabilities of your staff members permit.
- Delegate not only to your staff but also to other departments and service groups.
- Remember the 6 W Rules of Delegation:

  What has to be done?
  Who should do it?
  Why should it be done?
  In what way should it be done?
  With what should it be done?
  By when must it be done?

- To delegate effectively, you have to organize your own work well. You need to plan to delegate certain tasks, and then you have to supervise all delegated tasks and their deadlines by means of a control list.
- The extent to which your staff members cooperate in the delegation process is a measure of your effectiveness as a manager; this is known as leadership by delegation.
- Keep in mind that your staff members will have a positive feeling if you delegate a lot; this means you need to practice management by delegation.

Next, you should analyze this chapter in terms of your own goals and purposes:

- What seemed most important to me in the chapter?
- What new insights did I gain?
- What aspects of the chapter do I need to examine in more detail?
- What ideas do I want to put into practice?

Analysis of Chapter 3

Result No.	Pages	Ideas, Suggestions, Topics of Value	Target Dates for Attainment	Control

Ask yourself again and again, "How can I best use my time at this very moment?" Set your priorities even if you only have 10 minutes in which to do so!

CHAPTER 4

ACTUALIZING AND ORGANIZING: HOW TO TAKE CHARGE OF YOUR DAILY ACTIVITIES

One should never have so much to do
that there is no time left for thinking.

William M. Jeffers

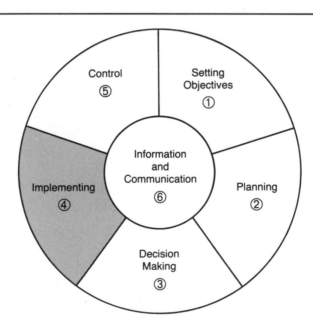

Course of a Typical Workday. It's the same problem almost every day. In the morning, at the beginning of your workday, you've planned a lot, maybe even made up a detailed activity list. But soon you are confronted, on the phone or in letters, with a variety of personal or business problems. And this is how it is going to be all day long. In the evening you will leave the office feeling that you have done a lot—but you don't quite know what you've achieved. This is what workdays often look like. However well you might have planned, after several unsuccessful attempts to take charge of daily events, you'll sooner or later find yourself back in a situation of stress and overwork.

It doesn't have to be that way, though. Experience shows that while some interruptions and distractions can't be eliminated completely, other disruptions are predictable and can be planned for. You can avoid a number of activities and idleness if you organize your day's activities and your work differently.

This chapter will give you practical advice on how to organize your daily work more efficiently.

4.1   PRINCIPLES OF ORGANIZATION

Organizing your work should be based on the following principle: I want to be in charge of my work, not the other way around. The following rules and principles should serve as suggestions for your daily planning, but they should not (and cannot) be binding recommendations. You may laugh at some of them, but they have proven to be worthwhile in a variety of work situations.

Evaluate each principle in terms of the degree to which:

- You're already following them, but want to intensify them.
- You want to try them.
- They don't apply to you.

It is important for you to find your *personal style;* there is no better one for you.

In terms of time, the 25 principles which follow can be divided into three groups:

Beginning of the Day	Course of the Day	End of the Day
1. _____	9. _____	21. _____
2. _____	10. _____	22. _____
3. _____	11. _____	23. _____
4. _____	12. _____	24. _____
5. _____	13. _____	25. _____
6. _____	14. _____	
7. _____	15. _____	
8. _____	16. _____	
	17. _____	
	18. _____	
	19. _____	
	20. _____	

1. Rules for the Beginning of the Day

1. Start Your Day in a Positive Mood. Try to see something positive in each day because your general attitude (e.g., how you want to tackle your tasks) plays an important part in your success or failure. Every morning, ask yourself these three questions:

- What can I do to have some fun with my work?
- How will this day take me closer to my goals?
- As a balance for work, what can I do for my health, e.g., fitness, relaxation, etc.?

And don't forget the following points:

- Whom will I meet today?
- To whom could I be of help?
- What difficulties and problems could I encounter today and how can I solve them in a positive way?

Take a couple of minutes each morning for yourself, before you start your standard morning program.

2. Have a Good Breakfast and Go to Work without Haste. A day you begin tired, unenthusiastic, maybe without a decent breakfast and rushing to the office can easily lead to failure.

Treat yourself to a substantial breakfast (energy for the whole day), and then drive calmly and without hurrying to work. Don't let other drivers bother you. Don't say, "I don't have time for that!" It's just a matter of priorities; getting up early means going to bed early.

3. Start your Workday Always at the Same Time. Start your daily work regularly—approximately at the same time. We are creatures of habit. Therefore, it is helpful for a lot of us to be at the office at a certain time every day. This way you can condition yourself to be ready for work at certain hours of the day.

4. Check Your Daily Plan. Take the plan you established the night before and check the planned activities and goals again according to their importance and immediacy and, if necessary, make corrections. Make a realistic plan for the whole day.

NOVEMBER	DECEMBER	JANUARY	Daily Plan	Wednesday
S M T W T F S	S M T W T F S	S M T W T F S		**13**
1 2 3 4	1 2	1 2 3 4 5 6		
5 6 7 8 9 10 11	3 4 5 6 7 8 9	7 8 9 10 11 12 13		
12 13 14 15 16 17 18	10 11 12 13 14 15 16	14 15 16 17 18 19 20		
19 20 21 22 23 24 25	17 18 19 20 21 22 23	21 22 23 24 25 26 27		
26 27 28 29 30	24 25 26 27 28 29 30	28 29 30 31	**Week 50 349/17**	**December 1989**
	31			

Most important task

⏱	Schedule	OK	✉📩 Contact	OK
8:				
9:				
10:				
11:				
12:				

5. Start the Most Important Task at the Beginning of the Day. Successful managers don't start with reading their mail first; they read it only after they finished several important tasks (A tasks). Very rarely does incoming mail contain matters of highest priority that have to be dealt with immediately. Therefore, start with your highest-priority task before reading the newspaper, before reading the mail, and possibly before your colleagues and staff start working.

6. Don't Waste Time Getting Your Work Started. You should refrain from such office morning rituals as extensive greetings, prolonged conversations on the latest news, events, or yesterday's TV program. Reschedule social contacts to times of lesser productivity, e.g., in the afternoon. This way you will save time for later interruptions and unforeseen activities.

7. Coordinate Your Time Plan with Your Secretary. It has been observed that "A good secretary doubles the effectiveness of her boss. A bad secretary cuts it in half." Your secretary is your most important partner when it comes to creating optimal working conditions. You should spend the first minutes of each workday with her or him, even if it's only a few minutes. Coordinate all deadlines, priorities, and daily goals with your secretary in advance. Later on, when you're busy with other matters, he or she will work more effectively and shield you from unnecessary disruptions.

8. Deal with Complicated and Important Matters in the Morning. After you've dealt with the most important matter of the day, turn to the second most important, and so on. You'll soon be taken up by the daily routine and various interruptions, anyway, so that you'll hardly be able to concentrate exclusively on your most important tasks. But in starting with the most complicated and important matters in the morning and staying with them consistently, you make sure that by the end of the day you will have finished or at least tackled them.

2. Rules for the Course of the Day

9. Be Well Prepared for Your Work. In the field of technology, the necessity and advantages of sufficiently planning work are undisputed; special "production planning" departments even exist for that purpose. In the business field, significant opportunities for "production planning" can be discovered, and time can be saved thereby (see Chapter 2.1). You can cut your actual work time by planning in advance.

10. Try to Adjust Deadlines. Deadlines are often accepted without any protest. But you should try to adjust deadlines that don't fit into your schedule very well by negotiating an alternative deadline. Often it's easier than you might think. Pay special attention to recurring meetings (e.g., daily or weekly meetings) so that they will come on a day or at a time that suits you.

11. Avoid Activities That May Have Bad Repercussions. Keep in mind the fact that actions taken by managers often produce bad results—results with a negative effect on those managers' ability to plan their time. How often—just as a result of participating in a single meeting—have you found yourself saddled with a set of new obligations? For example, you may have to confront yet another deadline or write up a status report, or even participate in a whole new project. Therefore, you need to check all your activities (such as appointments, talking to visitors, receiving telephone calls or letters) to see whether they are necessary or may lead to unwanted repercussions.

12. Decline Additional Pressing Tasks. There are always urgent cases and unexpected developments in every company and department. It often occurs that after you've dealt with the big problems, the small ones increasingly seem to push themselves to the forefront. Therefore, keep in mind that working on so-called urgent cases means neglecting your planned, important tasks, and will cost you time and energy. Try to refuse additional urgent cases if possible.

You should check to see:

- What losses you'll have to expect, if you ignore or postpone a particular matter.

- Whether your personal involvement is unavoidable.
- Whether the problem can be solved in any other way, e.g., by involving other people.

13. Avoid Unplanned, Impulsive Activities. If you suddenly want to do something else during work hours, e.g., to call someone, consider whether this interruption is necessary or useful for the task you're working on at the moment. Impulsively deviating from a plan usually decreases productivity since you can't keep to your priorities. But in working on a task you may often run into interesting ideas or important information that you might forget. Make a short note of the matter and work on it at a later, more suitable, time.

Of course, we don't want to suggest that you have to give up all spontaneous actions. Sometimes a spontaneous break or a talk with a colleague can be helpful and stimulating.

14. Take a Timely Break—Work at an Adequate Pace. How often and when do you take breaks? Working too long and too intensively doesn't pay since your concentration and productivity may drop off and mistakes may slip in. Don't think of breaks as a waste of time but as ways of relaxing and refueling your energy.

Take short breaks regularly.

Relax by stretching your legs, if possible in the fresh air.

Use longer breaks to improve your personal productivity, e.g., through a daily fitness program.

Take breaks in meetings, too. Often the most creative ideas emerge in such a relaxed atmosphere.

To achieve a regenerating effect from taking a break you need to take the break when your productivity is at its peak and before you have totally lost your concentration.

Try to observe this advice during meetings or in your daily work. Medical studies have shown that the best recreational effect can be achieved after one hour of work. The break should only last up to 10 minutes, since the optimal effect sets in within the first 10 minutes and declines after that.

Therefore take breaks of not more than 10 minutes, but take them more often within every hour. Let's think, for ex-

Productivity Curve within the Course of 60 Minutes

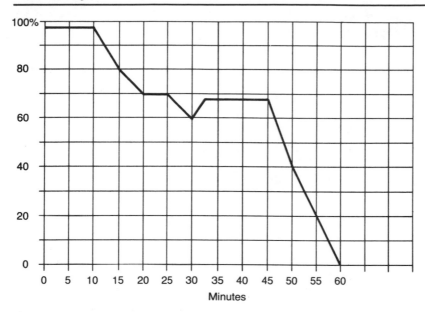

ample, of the Japanese companies that have made a successful practice of taking short breaks and fitness activities in groups.

Maintaining an adequate work pace is also important for maximum productivity. In the long run a hectic, hasty work style will require more effort and time than maintaining an average brisk pace—not to mention the repercussions of stress on your health.

15. Finish Smaller, Similar Tasks on a Mass-Production Basis. If you deal with short telephone calls, memos, letters, and meetings immediately or individually, you will lose a lot of time.

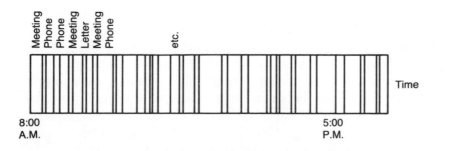

Instead, you should deal with routine tasks and odd jobs on a mass-production basis by concentrating similar tasks in work blocks:

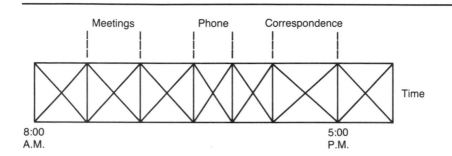

This has the important advantage of requiring you to prepare your activities only once and allowing you to stay with similar activities. Through concentrated and continuous work you'll save time. Six times 10 minutes of dictating letters, making telephone calls, explaining questions in short meetings, etc., will, if distributed over the entire day, be more disruptive than a time block of one times 60 minutes:

$$1 \times 60 \text{ minutes} < 6 \times 10 \text{ minutes}$$

In addition, you should accumulate in a work block all the reading material that you just want to glance over. Don't make your work blocks too long; you should keep them to between 30 and 60 minutes, since it might cause some irritation if, for example, your phone is constantly busy. Try to test the efficiency of the principle of mass production. Even if it saves only a few minutes a day, such time savings add up!

16. Finish Tasks That You've Already Begun. Once you get involved in a certain task, it will cost a lot of time to get back to it if you switch to other tasks in the meanwhile. This is because you will have to spend time retracing the last steps of your work. Furthermore, your creativity and ability to solve problems will be greatly reduced. Therefore, avoid jumping back and forth between tasks, and always try to finish tasks (or interrupt them at a suitable point). Allow enough time for a task. If there is a free period in your plan or in the last minutes before leaving your desk, start a task that you can finish within the time remaining. If you must interrupt your work, briefly write down ideas not yet elaborated, other suggestions, and everything else that could make it easier to start again on that job.

Keep in mind that there is no better way to deal with an A task than to sit down and work until it's finished.

17. Use Extra Bits of Time. Don't let superfluous or waiting time go by! You can even use the last minutes of your lunch break or the minutes remaining before closing time to plan, prepare, or take care of routine activities. By using extra bits of time productively, you'll gain time in the course of the week.

18. Work Countercyclically to Disturbances in the Office Routine. If possible, finish your most important tasks before noon. It's to your advantage to complete them before the office peak period, that is, the time when others are engaged in their main activities. As a result, you'll be able to work with fewer interruptions and more efficiently. In planning your day, therefore, take into account periods that are either low or high in disturbances. The following graph shows the distribution of disturbances that normally occur in an office day.

Graph of Daily Disturbances

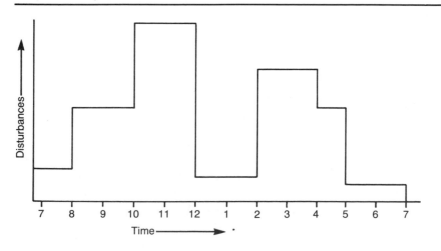

Using the Daily Disturbances form, make your own graph and compare it. The more aware you are of the work habits of your colleagues, staff, and business partners, the less susceptible you'll be to adding things spontaneously and being constantly interrupted. You work countercyclically if you:

- Finish your most important tasks during the quiet time before noon.
- Try to use your planned buffer time (40 percent) for C tasks during hours susceptible to interruptions, and try to handle such interruptions calmly.
- Don't read your mail in the morning, but postpone it for the time being.
- Come in earlier in the morning and leave earlier in the evening.

19. Establish a Quiet Hour.   In order to deal with the most important tasks, it is advisable for you to work with as few interruptions as possible. This is true, but how can we achieve it? In this connection it has proved worthwhile to arrange a "quiet hour" when you don't want to be disturbed by anybody. This is a very important appointment, maybe the most important of all: a one-hour appointment with *yourself.*

Note this appointment in your time planner just like a meeting with a visitor. A period of uninterrupted concentration will significantly increase your productivity. You can also use this time for important (but never pressing) tasks with long-term aspects (e.g., your continuing education), that often get lost in your day-to-day work. Isolate yourself during this quiet hour (with the help of your secretary), or close the door to your office, announcing that you're "not available." This might seem dishonest, but your most important tasks should have absolute priority at least once a day. You wouldn't be available if you had an important appointment either.

20. Monitor Your Time and Your Plans.   We tend to waste time early in meetings and on other tasks, thus leaving 80 percent of the agenda for only 20 percent of the remaining time. Set your watch for half time. When you buy your next watch, it should be one with a buzzer. In addition to checking your time, also check your plans several times a day in terms of accomplished tasks, new priorities, etc. This will enable you to adjust your planning to new conditions that have arisen in the course of the day. Planning has to be realistic (see rule number 4 on p. 107); otherwise, you'll be frustrated in the evening.

3. Rules for the End of the Day

21. Finish Odd Jobs. You should try to finish smaller jobs that you have accumulated during the day (such as reading the mail, dictating, or answering memos and letters) by the end of the day. Postponing them for another day or several days later can lead to an additional expenditure of energy, as you'll have to familiarize yourself with the tasks once again and deal with a bigger pile of unfinished business.

22. Monitor Results and Yourself. Comparing your goals with what you've actually achieved (in terms of your work or your personal life) should be an important part of how you structure your work. It should also include the next aspect of self-management, which we'll consider in Chapter 5.

23. Plan Your Time for the Next Day. Plan your next day the evening before. Check which tasks have not been completed and need to be transferred to the following day. Draw up a plan for it with the help of your time planner, including goals, priorities, and delegation (see the five-step method in Chapter 2.4).

24. Go Home in a Positive Mood. Look forward to a well-deserved evening off. Enjoy the ride home and get into the mood for the second part of your day. If possible work out regularly. A 10-minute workout each day in the fresh air, according to physicians, improves your physical condition.

25. Create a High Point Every Day. To lead a positive life, it is important for you to realize the value of each day in your life. It is not enough simply to check off accomplished tasks and successfully completed parts of your career goals, you should make every day a successful day. How can you create a high point every day? How about such activities as your family, the theater, music, reading, friends, going out, or meditation? What better possibilities for organizing your day do you know or practice?

1.
2.
3.
4.
5.

As you look back at this chapter; which principles of organization would you like to practice, improve, or try?

No.	Principle of Organization	When Accomplished

4.2 OUR NATURAL DAILY RHYTHM (THE PRODUCTIVITY CURVE)

Everyone's productivity is subject to changes that follow a natural rhythm. Some people are up at sunrise, some are grumpy all morning, others are night owls, and still others are too tired to do anything at night.

People in the first category work especially well in the morning, but are prone to getting tired earlier in the afternoon, and need to finish their workday earlier. Others get going in the late afternoon and like to work late at night. Neither of these groups works better or worse than the other—just differently. Their daily productivity has its ups and downs at different times. The average daily productivity capacity and its range of fluctuation or change are shown in the following graph.

Productivity Curve

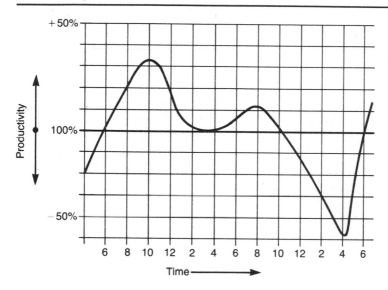

The 100 percent line indicates our average daily physiological productivity capacity. The curve shows fluctuations upward and downward, but the areas above and beneath the 100 percent line are equal in size. While the absolute peaks and downs are different for every individual, relative rhythmical fluctuation is common for all of us.

Phases of high activity are followed by two-hour relaxation periods, in which the body relaxes and shouldn't be strained excessively. What does that mean for your daily routine?

- The peak in productivity occurs before noon, when our stomach, pancreas, spleen, and heart are active in succession. This level won't be reached again within the course of the day. One more reason to start with the A tasks.
- After lunch, when the small intestines are active, the well-known low (which a lot of people try to fight with

coffee) sets in. Don't work against your biological rhythm; instead relax with a cup of tea and use this phase for social contacts and routine tasks (C tasks).

Everyone of use has to live with these fluctuations in personal productivity. Don't try to work against your natural daily rhythm (which you can change only minimally, anyway), but incorporate this regularity into your daily planning.

The curve of our average daily physical productivity has been tested on hundreds of thousands of people in all the industrial countries. Rejects, defect quotas, and the risks of accidents all run against our daily rhythms. For example, during the day the conveyer belts in auto production are accelerated or slowed down according to the productivity curve. There are different speeds for the night shifts and the day shifts.

The values of the normal curve do not necessarily have to correspond with your individual productivity. Everyone's productivity curve will deviate somewhat, possibly even very much, from the norm. Stimulants like coffee, tea, nicotine, or pills can accelerate the uplift in the morning, but also accelerate an afternoon low. Find your own daily rhythm. Establish your productivity curve through systematic observations. Observe yourself more consciously and ask yourself:

1. At what times of the day do I feel most productive, full of energy, and creative?
2. At what times am I very mentally alert?
3. At what times do I start to get tired; when are certain tasks difficult to do?
4. When do I feel burned out and tired?
5. When do I exercise, pursue my hobby, or relax?
6. At what time do I want to sleep at night, and when do I actually go to bed?

In this connection also ask:

7. When do I actually work?
8. When do I deal with my most important tasks and appointments?
9. When do I deal with less important tasks?

Record the results on the following form in your time planner over a 10-day period:

| Time | My Productivity | | | | | Compa-rison | My Actual Work Disposition | | |
	1 Creati-vity	2 Diffi-culties	3 Exhaustion	4 Balance	5 Desire for Sleep	6 Changes	7 Work Time	8 Impor-tant Tasks/ Appoint-ments	9 Less Important Tasks/ Appoint-ments
12 A.M.									
1 A.M.									
2 A.M.									
3 A.M.									
4 A.M.									
5 A.M.									
6 A.M.									
7 A.M.									
8 A.M.									
9 A.M.									
10 A.M.									
11 A.M.									
12 P.M.									
1 P.M.									
2 P.M.									
3 P.M.									
4 P.M.									
5 P.M.									
6 P.M.									
7 P.M.									
8 P.M.									
9 P.M.									
10 P.M.									
11 P.M.									
12 A.M.									

Now draw your own productivity curve:

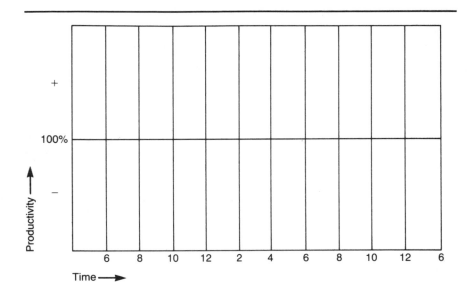

Compare the data of your productivity curve with the re-sults shown in columns 7 through 9. Then consider whether you can better coordinate your most important tasks, appoint-ments, and daily routine to meet your inner needs. Have a pos-itive attitude toward the active and quiet phases of your physiological productivity. Alternate, according to your inner rhythm, between demanding (that is, important) activities and relaxing (that is, less demanding) activities. Work daily on your productivity capability (exercise and your physical condition).

Always keep in mind that the quality of your work will change with your ability to be productive. Match the most im-portant tasks (A tasks) that involve high demands on concen-tration, quality, and productivity with the peak hours of your productivity curve, that is, with your best hours. Integrate your productivity curve into your overall daily planning. Work and live with—not against—your biological rhythms.

4.3 MANAGEMENT BY BIORHYTHM

Besides regular fluctuations in our daily productivity, we can observe other biological regularities over longer periods of time: *biorhythms*.

The theory of biorhythm is based on the idea that every human being's physical, psychological, and mental productivity is subject to rhythmic fluctuations that can be calculated in advance. The objective of biorhythmics is to identify our biological regularities or ups and downs, so that our activities can be planned accordingly. Management by biorhythm can be an effective tool for successful self-management.

Before proceeding a few explanations are necessary. Biorhythm theory has nothing to do with astrology, horoscopes, or fortune-telling. It is about the periodic recurrence of certain processes in the human organism. Applying biorhythm theory does not mean to align your life exclusively according to the biorhythm curve or to be afraid of the so-called caution days.

Rather, it suggests that we need to accept the fact that our productivity is influenced by recurring active and regenerative phases, and that we shouldn't try to live fighting against our "inner clock." The theory of biorhythm is based on the knowledge that the cells of the human organism are constantly being created and decomposing; they significantly influence our physical well-being, resistance, and energy. The building up and decomposing of our body's cells influences the nutrient supply of our blood—and therefore our energy potential.

1. The Three Biorhythms

Biorhythm theory is based on the assumption that every human being, from the time of birth, is influenced by three different, constantly changing streams of energy. The release of energy means activity (peak), while the absorption of energy implies relaxation (valley).

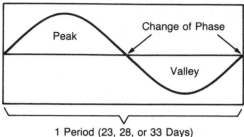

1 Period (23, 28, or 33 Days)

Three different rhythms can be distinguished: body rhythm, emotional rhythm, and mental rhythm.

B = Body Rhythm.   (Duration: 23 days; it changes every 11½ days.) Body rhythm affects all physical energies or energies that are driven by our own will.

E = Emotional Rhythm.   (Duration: 28 days; it changes every 14 days.) This rhythm affects our emotions, moods, and creative energies.

M = Mental Rhythm.   (Duration: 33 days; it changes every 16½ days.) This rhythm affects all mental abilities, e.g., concentration and presence of mind.

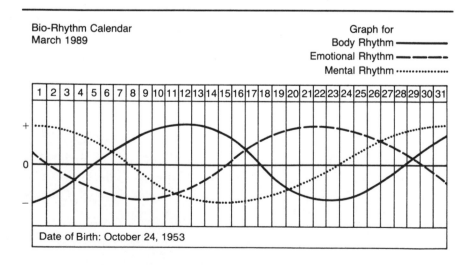

Since each of the three phases has a different duration, every human being constantly experiences changing combinations of physical, emotional, and mental well-being, or lack thereof.

Our example shows the biorhythmogram of a person born on October 24, 1953. The constant change between phases of energy build up $(-)$ and energy absorption $(+)$ in all three areas is clearly to be seen. These oscillations can be even more complex, e.g., after serious events (such as a major shock or surgery). Rhythm may shift and settle down only after a certain period of time has passed.

2.   Caution Days

Special attention should be paid to the transitional days when a rhythm graph changes from plus to minus or minus to plus (change of phase). They are called caution days, as sudden disruptions of bodily functions, productivity, will, or mental effort can occur. The change of phases takes 24 hours and, depending on the hour of birth, can extend into the preceding or following day. Important: Every caution period doesn't necessarily lead to a critical event (accident, mistakes, rash actions, disharmonies, etc.), but caution is advised.

As our organism switches over from activity (energy release) to relaxation (energy absorption) on such days, it is advisable not to waste our energies, but to use them economically, avoiding additional stress situations, such as surgery, vaccinations, emotional distress, excessive alcohol consumption, etc. Biorhythm is a natural phenomenon, and a healthy organism can easily deal with its fluctuations. There is no reason, therefore, to be afraid of caution days or valleys. On the other hand, we shouldn't underestimate to what degree an organism can be weakened during the transitional phase. On average, we have to deal with this additional risk factor every six days.

The following chart will supply you with an overview of all operational areas and effects of the three biorhythms in various phases:

Rhythm	Operational Area/Measuring Variables	Peak Energy Release	Valley Energy Absorption	Critical Time/ Unstable Condition
Body rhythm 23 days; change between peak and valley every 11.5 days	Physical condition, ability to take stress, well-being, strength, stamina, power of resistance, self-confidence, energy	Strength and stamina for physical activities (sports, work); favorable for travel, surgery, teeth extractions, resistance to illness	Quiet period, fatigue, reluctance to work, prone to illnesses, medications have good effects, sensitive to pain	Reluctance to work, discontent, aggressiveness, start or worsening of illnesses, extreme effects of alcohol consumption, physical damage
Emotional rhythm 28 days; change between peak and valley every 14 days	Emotional area disposition, the unconscious, capable of feelings, empathy, sociability, harmony, cooperation, moral strength, intuition, creativity, moods, self-control	Positive outlook on life, harmony, cooperation, favorable for exams, competition, public appearances, acquaintances, enjoyment in company	Negative emotions put pressure on teamwork and cooperation; watch interhuman relations; difficulties in making friends; monotony, depressions likely	Pointed remarks, pugnacity, frustration, worsening of illnesses, reduced reactions
Mental rhythm 33 days; change between peak and valley every 16.5 days	Intellectual area, the conscious, intellectual capacity, comprehension, adaptability, logic, judgment, attentiveness, reactions, mobility, memory (vitality, positive outlook on life)	Open-mindedness, open for new things; good memory, adaptability; favorable for new tasks, travel to foreign countries, studying of weak subjects, planning decisions, exams	Lack of concentration, deteriorating memory, lack of articulativeness; favorable for routine tasks, assembling and filing, repetition	Weak memory prone to make mistakes, rash mental actions, deterioration of attentiveness, presence of mind, and reactions; risk of accidents

3. The Importance and Uses of Biorhythms

The possibilities of using biorhythms are unlimited since you can apply them to every area of life: health, work, family and society, leisure, sports, etc. A number of Japanese and American companies, for example managed to reduce their accident rates by 30, 50, or nearly 60 percent within a short period of time through the use of this system.

Biorhythm can also help managers to plan. With the help of biorhythm theory we can prepare for the various fluctuations in personal productivity (depending on the kind and importance of the respective task), and so ensure better goal achievement through increased effectiveness. Through management by biorhythm we can read our inner clock, draw conclusions from that, and adjust to the natural fluctuations of our productivity in a positive way.

During valley or caution days, you should try to gain new energy, relax, spend your time on repetitive work, and avoid unpleasant people and problems. During peak days, go full speed ahead! Actively influence your fate: make decisions; carry out changes and rearrangements; and carry out your objectives.

Every individual's reactions to inner long-term biorhythms are different. In addition, a variety of other factors influence this rhythm sensitivity. In an industrial, high-performance society like ours, the automatic self-protection of our organism doesn't always work. Your body's signals, like listlessness, anxiety, increasing fatigue, etc., that are meant to indicate a reduced productivity (such as on caution days) and to protect you from overtaxing, are often suppressed by pressure from deadlines, stress, or—in persistent cases—by use of stimulants or tranquilizers. If for a long period of time the organism isn't able to fall back into its natural rhythm of activity and relaxation, then disorders, damage, breakdowns, and even death may occur. Therefore, consider your biorhythmic condition when planning and organizing your day—but don't overdo it.

How can I get my biorhythmogram? You can do so in the following ways: (1) through your own computations: you can find diagrams and advice in books on this subject; and (2) through electronic calculators: there are a variety of calculators and digital watches that have a built-in biorhythm function.

What *not* to do: After you've obtained your biorhythm data, it is absolutely wrong to euphorically watch your daily variables and internalize them. Biorhythmic data are like a weather report: Even if rain is predicted, the sun may shine. Biorhythmic curves only indicate tendencies that, based on functions in your organism, may occur. If your attitude is: "Today is a caution day, today I'll be miserable!", you'll probably be miserable because attitudes like this can influence our feelings and actions unconsciously and become a self-fulfilling prophecy.

Therefore, evaluate your data with caution. It may be useful at first to keep a "blind diary," where you note your physical, emotional, and mental condition; at the end of the week, you can compare these notes with your biodata. You can use your biorhythm data as a management tool (with some caution and skepticism), after you've developed a feeling for your biorhythm sensitivity and how it matches the curves.

Keep in mind that biorhythm influences our productivity—but it is just *one* factor.

4.4   YOUR PERSONAL WORK STYLE— HOW TO FREE UP YOUR TIME

Your personal work style is another factor which influences your daily work load and your success. It is determined primarily by your character, inclinations, and habits. Changes require you to be:

- Aware of strengths and weaknesses in terms of your work style.
- Motivated to preserve and consolidate the strengths.
- Willing to work on your weaknesses.

The following questions will help you examine your work habits. Please check those statements that come closest to your inclinations. You can also use the results from the Analysis of Time and Activities table in the Introduction.

Self-Evaluation: My Work Habits	Almost Never (0)	Some-times (1)	Often (2)	Almost Always (3)
Do you tend to:				
1. Procrastinate with unpleasant tasks?				
2. Postpone unpleasant but necessary decisions?				
3. Look for reassurance from others when it comes to unpleasant or difficult decisions?				
4. Do everything yourself?				
5. Work on several problems simultaneously?				
6. Work hastily?				
7. Tackle tasks before considering the best way to do it?				
8. Interrupt work to attend to other matters?				
9. Postpone difficult tasks after initially working on them?				
10. Work without much concentration?				
11. Work for two or more hours without a break?				
12. Not finish tasks, because you keep on getting interrupted?				
13. Use precious time for matters of secondary importance?				
14. Work on tasks that are not yours, only because they interest you?				
15. Take on tasks at any time, just because you can't say no?				
16. Tackle pointless cases, such as looking for the culprit of a mistake or fighting the administrative bureaucracy?				
17. Try to be perfect, even where it is unnecessary?				
18. Want to know all the facts?				
19. Take the initiative only after being induced to do so?				
20. Always want to help others with their work-related problems?				
Total Add up the columns and calculate your total point value				
	×0	×1	×2	×3
	=0	+	+	

=

The higher the point value, the more you're an obstacle to your own productivity.

1. Avoiding Time Wasters

On the following pages you'll find suggestions to help you overcome bad work habits that can cost you a lot of time. Record the actions you want to take on the form at the end of this chapter. You should view the improvement of your work techniques as a continuous process and be willing to continually respond to new suggestions and integrate them into your work habits.

Time Wasters: Causes and Countermeasures

Time Wasters	Possible Causes	Solutions
You're not setting goals or priorities; you have no plans.	You have no planning system. You're sometimes successful without planning. You think that each day is different and that unforeseen events can't be planned anyway. You're too action-oriented (action before thinking).	Buy a time planner. Keep in mind that planned activities more often lead to success than unplanned activities. Keep in mind that managers waste time in the same way over and over again; planning creates free time for unforeseen events and really important activities. Those who know why they're doing something are even more successful
You're trying to do too many things at a time.	You have no time planning. You concentrate on pressing issues. Your interests are too far-reaching.	Establish goals and priorities; plan your time. Focus on important issues. Focus on what is essential (less is more!).
Indecision.	You're afraid to make mistakes. Your decision-making process is irrational. Perfectionism: you want to know all the facts. You're lacking initiative and motivation.	You'll have to see that you can learn out of every mistake. Add up the facts, set goals and test alternatives; use proven decision-making techniques and follow decisions through.

Time Wasters—*Continued*

Time Wasters	Possible Causes	Solutions
Indecision. (cont.)		Accept risks as unavoidable; make decisions without knowing all the facts; a mediocre decision is better than none.
		Find the reasons for your dissatisfaction (attitude toward work, ambition, boss, staff, etc.).
Haste, impatience.	You have no planning. You don't evaluate your tasks. You're trying to achieve too much in too short of a time. You're impatient when it comes to details.	Plan the evening before those tasks that have to be finished by the next day (time planner). Differentiate between pressing and important task and make a priority list. Do less and delegate more (Eisenhower principle). Finish a task consistently so that you won't have to start over again or make revisions.
Inability to say no.	You're afraid to insult someone. You don't have ready excuses. You want to please, to be the always helpful colleague. You want to help others.	An honest answer doesn't have to be insulting. Example: "I'm sorry but I can't do it. But may I suggest the following. . . ." The best excuse is an honest one: say that you don't have time; it's understood that you plan your work daily and know how precious your time is. This is going to boomerang on you if you can't fulfill the expectations that people have of you; it can have negative effects. Don't overdo it; it will soon become expected of you.
You don't finish tasks.	You didn't set priorities. You didn't set deadlines. You're indecisive.	Set priorities according to importance and immediacy and finish tasks with highest priority first.

Time Wasters—*Concluded*

Time Wasters	Possible Causes	Solutions
You don't finish tasks. (cont.)		For all important tasks set realistic deadlines (daily plan) and keep them. See solutions under "Indecision."
You're disorganized.	You have no system. You're procrastinating. Everything lands on your desk. You're afraid you might lost track of things.	Write down everything important in your time planner and then file your documents. You really have to start with the important tasks first; give yourself deadlines. Instruct your secretary to sort out less important mail and to pass on to staff members requests that they can answer. With a time planner and the Overview form (see Chapter 6), you'll have a better overall view than if you'd stack everything on your desk; only keep those files on your desk that you really need.

2. Ways to Free Up Your Time

One of the most important requirements for a successful work style is to concentrate on the really essential and important issues and not to get lost in details. You can improve your work habits considerably and free up your time if you briefly question all of your tasks. The four successful liberating questions are:

- Why at all?
- Why me?
- Why now of all times?
- Why in this form?

Copy these questions onto an index card and place it on your desk where you can plainly see it. It will help you to keep away unnecessary work.

Why at All? Eliminate It!

- Is it absolutely necessary to go on this business trip, to read this report, to write this memo, etc.?
- Do I have to make an official memo about this procedure, keep this statistic regularly, read through all the incoming mail?
- Do I have to receive this visitor, take this call, answer this request?
- Do we really have to have a meeting? Do I have to take part in this meeting?

These and other questions will make you aware of the fact that some activities aren't really necessary or don't have to be dealt with in depth. Be more economical with your time budget, especially with less important matters.

Why Me?—Delegate it!

- Can this task be delegated or taken over by someone else?
- Am I really responsible?
- Am I not dealing with things here that don't concern me?
- Is this an attempt at reverse delegation?
- Does this correspond with my responsibilities and goals?

These questions should keep you from dealing with unnecessary tasks. Be more confident of your staff and use all possibilities to delegate. Rethink the distribution of goals, tasks, and authority between you and your staff.

Why Now of All Times?—Terminate It!

- What is the need for dealing with this task now?
- Is this task really pressing or can it wait?

- Wouldn't it make more sense to postpone this task to another date?
- Is this really the best time? (Remember your A tasks and the productivity curve.)

These questions should protect you from losing too much time by letting you choose the time to do a task. In terms of your daily plan, work with deadlines and try to define environment with precise time statements. For example, don't agree to statements like "before noon" or "on Friday." On the other hand, some things don't necessarily have to be finished, decided upon, or discussed "now" or "immediately."

Why in This Form?—Systematize It!

- Does a letter have to be answered with a time-consuming letter? (Why not call instead of dictating a letter?)
- Can I try out new ways of organizing, new techniques, or new means?
- How can I systematize and simplify this task even further?

These questions should suggest new ideas for organizing your work. If you continually question your old work habits and watch for new, creative, and systematic ways, you can often achieve considerable time savings.

4.5   YOUR DAILY ORGANIZER

Finally, with the help of the principles proposed in this chapter, you need to design a sample workday in this last exercise. Even if there will rarely ever be such an ideal day, you can use this model as an objective to achieve and to anchor your daily planning and organizing.

Make your daily organizer into a tool for designing your day. For example, think about the following topics:

- The start of the working day
- Your quiet hour
- The productivity curve
- Your breaks
- The curve of daily disturbances

- Monitoring your day
- Planning the next day

Use the form shown below and transfer it to your time planner. Using this exercise as a model, you can also make a weekly plan and practice distributing the various activities over the week. In creating your "ideal day" and "ideal week"

Daily Planner

Time	Tasks, Activities, Goals	Notes
5		
6		
7		
8		
9		
10		
11		
12		
1		
2		
3		
4		
5		
6		
7		
8		
9		
10		
11		
12		

you should also include private activities and goals, e.g., your family, sports, relaxing, cultural activities, friends, etc.

4.6 SUMMARY AND ANALYSIS

- The self-management functions of organizing and implementing enable you to methodically and systematically focus all your activities and energies on your goals.
- Organizing your workday means determining your own work and time to the extent possible, rather than having others determine them for you.
- The following checklist will supply you with a summary of the most important principles for organizing your day.
- In organizing your day, consider the fluctuations of your physiological productivity by arranging your tasks in accord with your own productivity peaks and valleys.
- Find out about your daily rhythm by systematically monitoring your productivity.
- Biorhythm shows the ups and downs of our vitality over longer periods of time (active, passive, or critical phases): it shows that period fluctuations in the physical, emotional, and mental areas exist, but it can't yet explain why.
- Your biorhythm shows general tendencies, but does not create events. You should consider your biorhythm when planning (even far in advance), and thus make it more likely that you'll achieve your goals.
- Scrutinize your work style and develop it further by integrating new suggestions, e.g., the elimination of time wasters or restricting habits.
- Look for possible improvements: there is always a simpler way to do things.

Principles for Organizing Your Day

Rules for the Beginning of the Day
1. Start your day in a positive mood.
2. Have a good breakfast and go to work without haste.
3. Start your workday always at the same time.

4. Check your daily plan.
5. Start the most important task at the beginning of the day.
6. Don't waste time getting your work started.
7. Coordinate your time plan with your secretary.
8. Deal with complicated and important matters in the morning.

Rules for the Course of the Day
9. Be well prepared for your work.
10. Try to adjust deadlines.
11. Avoid activities that may have bad repercussions.
12. Decline additional pressing tasks.
13. Avoid unplanned, impulsive activities.
14. Take a timely break—work at an adequate pace.
15. Finish smaller, similar task on a mass-production basis.
16. Finish tasks that you've already begun.
17. Use extra bits of time.
18. Work countercyclically to disturbances in the office routine.
19. Establish a quiet hour.
20. Monitor your time and your plans.

Rules for the End of the Day
21. Finish odd jobs.
22. Monitor results and yourself.
23. Plan your time for the next day.
24. Go home in a positive mood.
25. Create a high point every day.

Begin to question your tasks and look for ways to free up your time even more.

Liberating Questions	Actions
Why at all?	→ Eliminate
Why me?	→ Delegate
Why now of all times?	→ Terminate
Why in this form?	→ Systematize

Review this chapter with regard to your personal needs.

- As I was reading this chapter, what seemed especially important to me?
- What new insights have I gained?
- Were any assumptions of mine confirmed?
- What ideas do I want to put into practice?

Analysis of Chapter 4

Result No.	Pages	Ideas, Suggestions, Topics of Value	Target Dates for Attainment	Control

Protect your time and treat it as you would your money. Do things when you want to, not when others want you to!

CHAPTER 5

CONTROLLING: HOW TO SUCCESSFULLY IMPLEMENT YOUR PLANS

Control is better.

Lenin

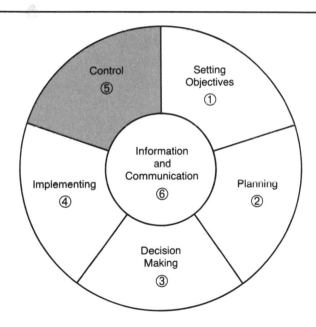

5.1 FUNCTIONS OF CONTROLLING

The last function in the circle of self-management is control, which is often seen as the main managerial activity. Controlling—which means the comparison between expected and actual results—promotes improvements in the self-management process. Controls show if your goals have been achieved, and they also initiate corrections.

Setting goals and planning are only as good as the subsequent implementation and control of those plans. So, therefore, regularly monitor the implementation of your plans. Mistakes and imperfect actions allow you to learn and gain more experience.

Controlling consists of three tasks:

1. Monitoring the actual situation. What have I achieved up to now?
2. Comparing what you expected to do and what you actually did. To what extent have I achieved my goal?
3. Taking corrective measures in case of 🌑 divergence from your goal. How can I bring the results closer to my original expectation?

The timing, duration, and frequency of controls depend on the nature of the tasks and the goal. Here we can differentiate between (1) controlling the processes and activities and (2) controlling the result or goal.

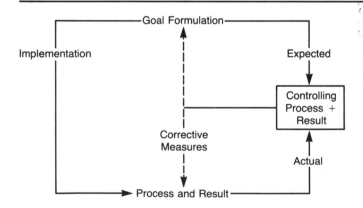

5.2   CONTROLLING ROUTINES (PROCESSES)

You should check your plans and the organization of your work at regular intervals. For example, during the course of the day, repeatedly ask yourself, if you're really:

- Working only on tasks that are necessary and worthwhile.
- Tackling tasks in the order of their priority.
- Finishing tasks within the planned time limit.
- Delegating enough, even tasks that are pressing.
- Grouping smaller tasks such as telephone calls and dictation of correspondence in a single work period.
- Fighting interruptions and time wasters.

You should also regularly make use of the Analysis of Time and Activities and the list of Distractions and Interruptions so as to be able to control and improve your personal work style. (You'll find these forms on page 7 in the Introduction to this book.)

The results will help you to detect and counteract unnecessary time wasters—bad habits that you may have come to enjoy, such as telephone conversations, preparing unnecessary reports, superfluous or lengthy meetings, unpleasant interruptions, mixed-up priorities, inadequate delegation, and similar problems. There are no better aids to controlling than the forms mentioned above. They'll begin to help as soon as you start to complete them in a conscientious way.

1.   Controlling by Means of the Analysis of Time and Activities Form

Controlling by using this form involves comparing the actual to the expected use of your work hours in a day or a week:

Analysis of Time and Activities

Actual	Expected	

(diagram: Actual column with several blank lines summing to Σ Hrs.; Expected column blank area with a line summing to Σ Hrs., and "Gained Hrs."; bracket pointing to list)

Tasks That
Could Be:
• Eliminated
• Delegated
• Terminated
• Systematized

We propose the following system for making use of this form. First, you should write down the important or A tasks you would tackle if you had one more hour a day at your disposal. List your goals or expected activities below:

1.
2.
3.
4.

Second, write in the "actual account" column below all your daily and weekly activities. For now, you only need to record these activities and how much time you spend on each:

Actual Account	Actual Time (hrs./mins.)		Expected Account	Expected Time (hrs./mins.)	
	Daily	Weekly		Daily	Weekly
List of recurring daily/weekly activities			List of time-saving possibilities		

Third, complete the "expected account" column by analyzing each activity in the "actual account" column with a view to ways of saving time. What would happen if you:

- Eliminated this particular activity?
- Delegated this activity or parts of it?
- Finished this activity in a shorter time period (e.g., in half the time)?

If nothing or only very little would happen, then how can you eliminate this activity, delegate it, or finish it in a shorter time period? You should enter these measures in the "expected account" column and establish new times or dates.

Finally, compare what you actually did with what you expected to do. Ask yourself:

- How much time do I currently spend on this task (that is, how much actual time is involved)?
- What is the expected time?
- How much time can I save?
- What is the percentage of potential time-saving?
- What time-saving measures should I introduce?
- How should I use the time that's been saved in a sensible way?

Check your activities constantly—or at least on a regular basis—with a view to ways in which you might save time and energy.

2. Controlling by Analyzing Daily Disturbances

By analyzing your daily disturbances you can discover further ways to save time. In the table that follows write down your activities and interruptions as well as possible ways to improve and correct the situation.

Actual Time				Expected time
From–To	Interrupted Activity	Interruption Phone Visitor	Duration of Interruption	Corrections and Possibilities for Improvement

You can derive new ways of correcting and improving your work process from this analysis. Later you can compare them with the implementation.

5.3   CONTROLLING RESULTS

The logic of the self-management process is based on achieving your goals at the end of the planning period. After finishing your tasks you should examine the results in terms of goal achievement (outcome control). For bigger projects you should also regularly examine the process itself (process control).

Regularly monitor, therefore, your yearly, monthly, weekly, and daily plans. Ask yourself:

- Which of the tasks have I finished?
- What were the results?
- What did I leave unfinished and why? (Note also such reasons as interruptions.)
- Where did I waste time (process control)?
- What conclusions do I draw for planning the next period (day, week, or month)?

Keep in mind that you have to plan and carry out your tasks and controls early on if you want to be in a position to make the necessary corrections. For complex tasks you should make a control list and then transfer the deadlines to your time planner.

Control List

No.	Task	Deadlines	Expected Results	Actual Results	Reasons for Deviations	Action Taken

5.4 LOOKING BACK ON YOUR DAY (SELF-CONTROL)

At the end of the day you should examine not only the results of your tasks but also your personal situation. In doing so, examine what went right or what could have been done better. The following suggestions will help you examine your situation:

Looking Back on Your Day
- Who or what hindered my performance today?
- Where did I get stuck in details?
- Where did I criticize someone negatively?
- Where did I make careless compromises?
- Where did my excessive ambition lead me to demand too much from others?
- What could the company justly ask from me?
- How would I evaluate myself if I were my colleague, my boss, or my subordinate?
- What activities could I have left undone?
- What did I learn today?
- Did I write down my ideas or work on them?
- What gave me pleasure?
- Did I come closer to achieving my goals today?
- What is the nicest thing I could do today?

Experience shows, though, that you'll probably use such an extensive list only irregularly or not at all. The following five-step checklist will help you find the right questions:

1. *Experience:* What experiences or insights did I have today?
2. *Goals:* What did I achieve today?
3. *Advice:* How did I help others or make them happy?
4. *Mental condition:* What was my predominant mood today?
5. *Physical condition:* What was my physical condition today? What did I do for my health?

You can also evaluate each day in the following way, noting it in your time planner:

A = an exceptional day

B = a very good day

C = satisfying

D = a bad day

In evaluating your day, emphasize its value with a positive attitude. If you have a bad day, noting it can also highlight the good days, and your mood can improve.

5.5   SUMMARY AND ANALYSIS

If you want to liberate yourself effectively, you can't do without self-control. Even a small sense of achievement will have a positive effect on your mood and motivation, and will strengthen the development of your work style.

Finally, analyze this chapter for your personal use.

• What seemed particularly important to me?
• What particular new insights did I gain?
• What did I find that confirmed my own insights?
• What area would I like to work on in detail?
• What do I want to translate into action?

Analysis of Chapter

Result No.	Pages	Ideas, Suggestions, Topics of Value	Target Dates for Attainment	Control

CHAPTER 6

INFORMATION AND COMMUNICATION: HOW BEST TO DEAL WITH MEETINGS, TELEPHONE CALLS, AND CORRESPONDENCE

Do it now—do it wrong—do it again!

A participant in a seminar

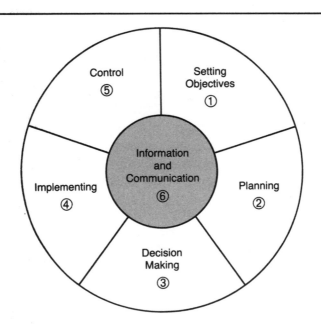

6.1 IMPORTANCE OF INFORMATION AND COMMUNICATION

The area of information and communication is in the center of the self-management diagram; all other functions revolve around it. Day in and day out we are overwhelmed by a flood of information that we have to confront.

Processing information should be done in a systematic and organized manner, with your career and personal goals in mind. Ideally, you should only have to deal with information important in solving your problems and achieving your goals. A strict orientation toward goals can serve to screen information so that goal-relevant data are automatically perceived as more important than data of only minor value. However, in most situations, you have to accept, process, and pass on more information than is actually necessary.

The area of information and communication serves as an important link between the other self-management activities since you have to constantly exchange information and to communicate. Communication is the exchange of information. Together, information and communication are the major functions of management relationships, social systems, and life in general. Managers spend on average 80 percent of their time on reading, correspondence, telephone calls, meetings, and so forth.

How much of your time do you spend on information and communication? Percentage of time: _____ percent. As you keep this fact in mind, take a look at your daily analysis of time and activities.

Roughly half of all information circulating in a company is superfluous—but which half? This chapter focuses on helping a company manager to efficiently process information and communication. Since an abundant literature exists on this topic, it would be beyond the scope of this book to discuss its many facets in detail. We will, therefore, restrict ourselves to short surveys and summaries.

6.2 EFFICIENT READING

The flood of reading material we're exposed to every day in the form of letters, newspapers, journals, memos, etc. becomes more and more overwhelming. Managers spend roughly 30 percent of their time just reading. Improving your reading technique, therefore, means also improving your working technique. Efficient reading helps you to better process the flood of information; reading without a system is a waste of time and money.

There are three different techniques or forms of efficient reading. These relate to the time aspect: (1) before reading, (2) during reading, and (3) after reading. Robinson's SQ 3R method deals with all three phases:

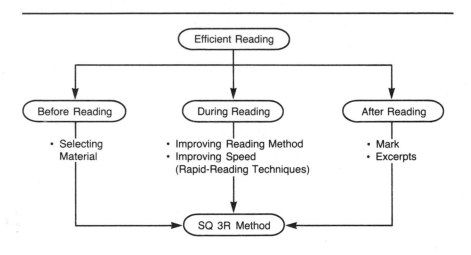

1. Before Reading

Before you start reading you should decide what parts of the text in front of you (book, newspaper, article, or memo) are—in terms of your personal career goals—of significant interest. Regardless of your reading speed, you can save a considerable amount of time through selective reading. Therefore, choose to read only the information that is absolutely necessary to you.

How can you read 200 pages in one minute? It's very simple: all you have to do is use this minute to look through the table of contents and decide that this 200-page book is not for you. A critical analysis of what some of us read daily would show that a lot of it doesn't need to be read. Reading efficiently, therefore, means first selecting and deciding if you want to read something at all; and if you do, how much of it you want to read.

The following questions should prompt you to understand reading less as a spontaneous, emotionally regulated act (e.g., throwing yourself with curiosity onto incoming mail) than as a rational process:

- What do I have to read?
- What should I read?
- What do I want to read?
- What do I want to do with it?
- What could I read later?
- What don't I have to read at all?

Always keep in mind that you have to pay money for some of the items you read (books, magazines, etc.), but that you also have to pay with time for each and every one of them. How much time per day or week do you actually have at your disposal to read all you have to read and all you want to read? Economize on your reading time and make a conscious choice from the reading material on hand according to the following decisional design.

Select and examine the material before you read it—or don't read it at all.

Group together smaller documents to read in a block of time, and reserve at least one hour a week for reading.

2. During Reading

After you've made your first, positive decision (i.e. to take a closer look at a text), you can—depending on your goals—continue by using the following methods:

- *Orienting.* Try to get an idea what the text is about—examine the contents—to see what is awaiting the

Checkup for Reading

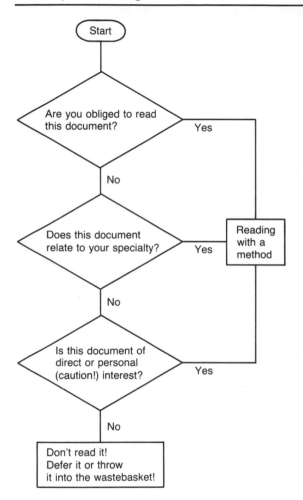

reader. This is the last test before deciding whether to read the text or not.

- *Scrutinizing*.   Look for the basic message, ask questions, and analyze the text. Find out what information is more important, less important, or unimportant.

• *Summarizing.* Make a summary of the content and critically analyze it. Note the central ideas.

Be goal-oriented in trying to read only what is most important.

Ten Ways to Improve Your Reading Method

1. While examining and reading a text, think about what information you want to extract from this work now and in the future.
2. Look at the title and subtitle and glance through any abstracts. Read the preface and introduction, too, since they will give you an idea of what the text is about.
3. Decide what you want to read intensively. When glancing through the paragraphs, look for key sentences, concluding words, or key words.
4. Skip the marginal notes, any small print, annotations, statistics, appendixes, extensive descriptions, and passages where the author may deviate from the subject.
5. Follow the author's train of thought rather than the exact words of the text. Try to find the individual and general ideas.
6. Look for indicators of thought, such as headings, underlined passages, indented sentences, and tables.
7. Word indicators signal introductory, intensified, or stressed passages of a text:

   • Opening signals such as *therefore, consequently, provided that,* etc. introduce fundamental or explanatory thoughts. It makes sense here to read the preceding and following sentences as well.
   • Intensifying signals such as *also, as well, besides, further, furthermore,* etc. stress a thought that previously was briefly mentioned.
   • Change-signals such as *but, apart from the fact that, on the other hand, either-or, on the contrary, although, instead, despite, rather,* etc. indicate that the direction or tendency of thought is changing.

8. Glance through passages that obviously contain less information, and slow down when reading important passages.
9. When reading a variety of documents, also consider their different structures:

   - The news in newspapers and magazines presents the most important information at the beginning and matters of secondary importance at the end.
   - Comments and statements provide essential information, i.e., the author's conclusion, in the last paragraph.
   - Specialist articles contain an abstract (a description of the problem), a main section (the solving of the problem), and a conclusion (a summary and/or discussion).

10. Improve the processing of the reading material by afterwards assessing your work (marking the text or making excerpts).

In addition to improving your reading method, you can also improve your reading speed. Without rapid-reading training an adult can read on the average 200 to 250 words per minute; after mastering the respective techniques, you can read roughly 400 to 500 or more. Furthermore, an improved and perfected reading technique will not only increase your reading speed but also your concentration and comprehension (understanding of contents and recollection) of texts.

These arguments should convince you to take part in a month-long quick-reading course, either in a seminar setting or at home by yourself. If you practice regularly for half an hour a day, it should take you only a month to increase your reading speed. You can learn to read faster by (1) reducing bad habits, and (2) using better methods.

Reading Faster by Reducing Bad Habits. The basis for rapid-reading techniques is to reduce old, bad habits that average readers have acquired over time and that prevent them from reading faster and more systematically:

Eight Interference Factors

1. *Reading letter by letter or syllable by syllable.* If your eye slowly moves from letter to letter or from syllable to syllable, each of these signs will become a fixation, your reading will falter, and your speed will be low. It should be your goal to grasp several words at a glance. Normally you can identify a word by a few letters only.

2. *Vocalizing.* The flow of reading will be extensively reduced if you have the habit of reading the text aloud or vocalizing it internally. Therefore, keep your lips closed. Your goal should be to grasp several word clusters and their meaning with one blink of your eyes.

3. *Going back to preceding passages (regression).* If your eyes wander back and forth to already read passages, you will increase the text volume and decrease your reading speed.

4. *Superficial reading.* A lack of concentration and/or lack of interest may cause you to read a text without understanding its meaning and the information contained in it.

5. *Following the text with your finger or with a pencil.*

6. *Moving your head instead of your eyes.* Your eyes can move much more quickly.

7. *An uncomfortable reading position.* You shouldn't read while lying down—you'll quickly get tired and your concentration will decline.

8. *A poor reading environment.* Insufficient light, distractions, and noise have a negative impact.

If you want to increase your reading speed, you will have to get rid of bad habits and distractions.

Reading Faster through Better Methods: Read More in Less Time. We often hear—and wrongly so—about "diagonal reading." We strongly advise against this method: by reading diagonally only a very small part of the text can be perceived so that important passages are totally out of your field of vision.

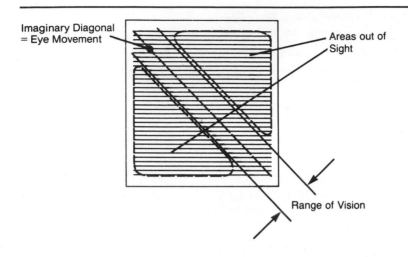

The slalom technique, shown below, seems more sensible.

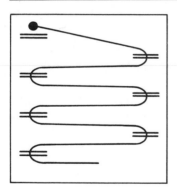

Here, the fixation points are word groups (key words).

A course in rapid reading will help you double or triple your reading capability through exercises such as these:

- Reducing bad habits
- Antiregression training
- Eye gymnastics

- Concentration exercise
- Normalization of vision range
- Jump-reading exercises

In particular, you'll learn peripheral reading; that is, reading with a broader range of vision that allows you to read faster and also to better understand the text. With a broader range of vision you'll be able to better grasp larger word groups, and you'll understand better what you're reading. A prime example of a rapid reader is the late President John F. Kennedy, who could read up to 1,200 words per minute!

3. After Reading

Make it a habit to not only read important texts but also to assess them afterward. By marking important passages and making excerpts, you'll make sure that you have read the text thoroughly. You'll also make it easier to reread the text if you need to do so.

Marking a Text. The objectives and advantages of marking a text are:

- You're setting priorities; important passages will be emphasized and unimportant passages will be de-emphasized.
- You will add structure to a text.
- You will make it easier to find and reread important passages.
- You will make it easier to concentrate on your train of thought, to better understand it, and to remember it.

Examples of marking techniques are underlining, marginal notes, and highlighting. Fluorescent highlighters are highly popular today. Their advantage is that they cover and visualize the whole word group, making it easier to look through a text again. Connecting lines between words highlight associations. The most effective technique (next to highlighters) is using symbols that you make while reading. You can develop your own *marcoglyphics*. Here is a sample:

!	= important
!!	= very important
?	= doubtful
0̸	= average
→	= reexamine
∇	= attention
E	= example
Σ	= summary
N	= name
)∈	= contradiction
ⓔ	= excerpts
ic	= index card
ⓧ	= make photocopies
⋈	= outdated theory
⋈	= new theory

Don't hesitate to mark your books and reading material in this way. Books—with the exception of rare books—are basic commodities. Only after you've intensively marked a book or text with underlined passages or notes will it become valuable. Once you get used to a specific marking system, stay with it and use it regularly. Mark your text sparingly but purposefully.

Making Excerpts.   While marking emphasizes textual passages, creating excerpts can extract important ideas. It is an obvious technique in cases where you can work better with abstracts (e.g., presentations, articles, long papers). The basic principle for making excerpts is to extract in short form only what is essential.

There are three forms of excerpts:

1. Excerpts that are transcribed verbatim. Here you'll have to follow official rules for quotations (naming

Example

Efficient Reading	Key Word
Excerpts on Bookmarks	Title
"A practice that has been proven valuable is making excerpts on bookmarks, using strips of cardboard about half a page wide and a little longer than a book page, so that they stick out of the closed book. The bookmark is placed along-side the page, and the excerpt is written on the bookmark at the height of the respective passage. Since space is limited, you'll have to be very selective and brief. It is best to work with structural excerpts here. Instead of cardboard strips, you can also use index cards that can later be used to establish an excerpt file. Colors can be used to signify different topics and projects."	(2nd Key Word)
	Quote
Source: Zielke, Wolfgang. *Handbook of Learning, Thinking and Working Techniques*, Munich, 1980, p. 223.	Source

source, etc.). This is indispensable for presentations, manuscripts, and research papers. But keep in mind that photocopying can save more time than writing excerpts by hand.

2. **Excerpts that are paraphrased.** In this case you present the author's ideas in your own words. In research papers you must identify these passages. The same rules as with literal quotations apply here.

3. **Excerpts that are summarized.** Here you'll summarize the most important points, theories, ideas and suggestions from a longer text onto a few sheets. If you need to search for specific passages later, this summary will be a valuable reminder. You can also add your own ideas and remarks.

Here is an example of a form you can use for a book excerpt:

	Effficient Excerpting of Books		
Book (Bibliographic Details)			Location
Pages	Ideas, Topics, Suggestions	Until When?	Control

Instead of following the order of the text, you can also make a summary according to the logical structure. The advantages of this reading method are:

The overall context is presented correctly.

Redundancies are avoided as repetitive words, articles, or details are omitted.

Information can be recalled visually and more easily memorized

Key words help in associating details for later reviews.

Structural Excerpt (Example)

Although there is almost no researcher who accepts Dänikens theories on extraterrestrial life, the question remains interesting and can't be easily dismissed. For a long time human beings have claimed to be the only intelligent beings in the universe. Today humans consider it highly probable that extraterrestrial life exists. In 1969 and 1973 the world press circulated reports that the Russian researcher Petrov received signals from outer space. Before that, we had been ready to admit that plants and animals could exist on other planets just like on Earth, but now human beings also seemed to exist. The attention over these observations died down. But again there are fantastic reports on UFOs that have been allegedly sighted. None of these objects have been proven to be vehicles from outer space, just as the sagas of our ancestors about far-away gods can't be considered authentic reports. But maybe simple reasoning will lead us to believe that life outside of our solar system must exist. The Earth belongs to this solar system, but the latter is only part of a bigger order, the galaxy or Milky Way. The galaxy exists in a big spirallike accumulation of stars. Its dimensions are almost incomprehensible. One estimates a diameter of 80,000 light years and a height of 16,000 light years. Nevertheless, there are millions of other similar systems, that are immeasurable distances away from this galaxy. But let us stay in this galaxy. Given the large number of solar systems in this galaxy, the number of planets has been conservatively estimated at 1 million. A spectral analysis has proven that even in faraway worlds there are no other substances than the roughly one hundred that we know. Considering these numbers, is it therefore unthinkable that many planets exist that are similar to Earth? On the contrary, it is absolutely probable that a greater number of similar celestial bodies exist. Apart from this one can imagine the existence of creatures that survive without oxygen—similar to creatures in the deep mud on the bottom of some oceans. It seems obvious that there is life, even intelligent life, all over the universe.[1]

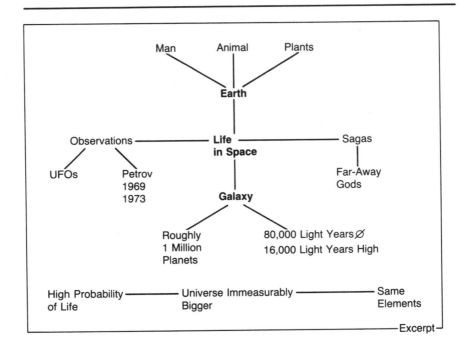

Another kind of excerpt can provide a summary of where certain topics are dealt with in different books. Noting the page numbers will make it easier to find the various passages. An example follows:

---

[1]Wolfgang Zielke, *Handbook of Learning, Thinking, and Working Techniques* (Munich: Modern Industry, 1980), p. 232.

Main Topics \ Authors	Wendt-Nordahl (1978)	Müller-Welser (19770	Niessler (1978)	Paul (1977)	Pohl (1978)
1. Organizational theory	pp. 66–85	pp. 39–48			
Traditional	pp. 66–70	pp. 39–42			
Modern	pp. 70–85	pp. 42–48		pp. 37–102 pp. 332–96	pp. 14–35
2. Principles of participation	pp. 3–54	pp. 17–38			
Term, forms, levels	pp. 12–15, 96–106	pp. 17–20, 28–33		pp. 217–48	
Laws	pp. 37–54	pp. 21–28, 33–35		pp. 397–414	
3. Interests of employees	pp. 85–93		pp. 23– 27	pp 362–65	pp. 10–58
4. Participation and goal development	pp. 57–66				
Goal relations (conflicts)		pp. 33–66	pp. 1–118		
Power	pp. 22-27	pp. 53–62	pp. 7–43, 89–105		
			pp. 44–87	pp. 58–62, 173–81, 286–310	
5. Participation and goal achievement		pp. 67–91	pp. 119–57		
Company politics, general	pp. 106–57	pp. 86–91	pp. 129–38		pp. 59–60, 130–35, 159–70
Finance policy, accounting	pp. 157–255	pp. 73–86			
Personnel policy	pp. 256–79, 269–79	pp. 67–73	pp. 120–28, 216–331	pp. 103–215	pp. 87–170

Just as with marking techniques, there are also many creative ways to develop excerpts. These include point-of-view excerpts, key-word excerpts, excerpts spoken on tape, and combinations of these types.

Develop your own excerpt system. Here again it is best to stay with a system once started. This way you can start an archive or excerpt file of important publications in your field. You can use index cards, sheets of loose-leaf paper, or photocopies that you can file in index card boxes or file cabinets. Make excerpts of the most important information and file it for later purposes. But try to set priorities here, too.

4. The SQ 3R Method

The principles of the following "3-step" or "5-step method" can serve as an overview of efficient reading, with which you can efficiently process a book article. This method was developed by F. Robinson and is sometimes also called the SQ 3R method:

```
S = Survey       ⎫
Q = Question     ⎬ Three-step  ⎫
R = Read         ⎭ method      ⎬ Five-step
R = Recapitulate              ⎪ method
R = Review                    ⎭
```

This is what the five steps mean in detail:

1. Survey. First you should generally get acquainted with the information of the book. After examining the preface and introduction, table of contents and text on the cover, headings of chapters and subheadings, summaries and stream-of-consciousness plans, and indexes and glossaries, you'll be ready to evaluate the reading material and decide whether to read the book or which parts of it. By doing so, you can save a lot of time, enabling you to read a chapter or article page for page.

2. Question. In order to critically examine or work through your reading material, it is insufficient to read passively and just absorb information. Active reading entails questioning the text, which helps reading and memorizing by increasing attentiveness. As you read, ask yourself:

- Is it new or already known information?
- Is it a fact, an opinion, or a hypothesis?
- Where are important passages?
- What is the author's intention?
- Where do I agree or disagree?
- With what previous knowledge can I compare this reading material?
- Where does this text differ from my previous knowledge?
- Does this material induce action on my part?

Questioning the text enables you to separate essential from nonessential parts, and makes you read more critically and with concentration; you won't have to read the text a second time.

3. Read. The next step deals with the absorption of the reading material. Here again you can use previously mentioned means such as underlining, highlighting, structuring, graphics, key words, etc. We advise you to use the above-mentioned rapid-reading techniques. If you're working through important reading material, you should also use the next two steps of the five-step-method:

4. Recapitulate. Recapitulate the text once again to make sure that the material has been understood. Here the questions under No. 2 (above) will be of great help. Changing from questioning to reading to recapitulating will keep up your motivation and delay any fatigue.

5. Review. In reviewing the material at the end, you should summarize individual findings, complete your notes, and ensure results by making excerpts. Here again it makes sense to make sure that you've understood the contents by reviewing the most important questions and answers.

Even though the SQ 3R method takes some getting used to, questioning the text will later become quite natural. Efficient reading can also induce multiple readings of the same material, in which each reading serves a different purpose:

- *1st reading:* selecting the material—deciding on the next steps.
- *2nd reading:* scrutinizing or summarizing what you've read.
- *3rd reading:* intensive (rapid) reading with marking.
- *4th reading:* recapitulation in order to review goals and questions.
- *5th reading:* rereading and making excerpts.

6.3   EFFICIENT MEETINGS

Meetings absorb the greatest part of a manager's activity and time. Surveys have shown that managers, depending on their level, spend 50 to 80 percent of their time at conferences and meetings. No other activity wastes so much time for so many people as meetings do. Try to calculate the costs of a two-hour meeting of 10 managers on the upper management level:

Our Calculation

	$	100,000	Yearly income (gross)
+	$	80,000	Fringe benefits (77.5%)
=	$	180,000	x 10 participants
=	$ 1,800,000		: 200 (effective workdays in the company)
=	$	9,000	Costs of one workday (10 participants)
=	$	2,250	: 4 (costs for two hours)

Try to make a cost-benefit analysis of your next meeting:

- Preparation costs
- Salaries of participants
- Fringe benefits (about 77.5 percent)
- Expenses (traveling)
- Lost time and production

Depending on the level of participants and size of the meeting, it can cost *hundreds of dollars a minute.* So why do we waste so much time and money on meetings? The reason is that many meetings are insufficiently prepared and organized, poorly managed, or insufficiently evaluated. Most meetings take too long and are basically superfluous.

The following 25 rules provide suggestions for preparing, managing, and evaluating meetings efficiently.

1.   Before the Meeting

1. "The best meetings are those that don't have to take place." You should always keep this sentence in mind

when deciding on whether to call a meeting. Personal meetings are worthwhile in situations requiring the following:

- Exchange of information.
- Pooling of ideas and opinions.
- Analyzing difficult situations and problems.
- Decision making in complex situations.

Working in groups can be more efficient than individual work, but it generally takes up more time.

2. Think of the alternatives to calling a meeting:

- Decision by manager in charge.
- Several individual phone calls or a conference call.
- Combining one meeting with another.

3. Find out if you have to take part personally:

- Is it possible to cancel without missing anything?
- Is it possible to send a representative?

4. Limit your participation to the extent it is needed.
5. Restrict the number of participants. Only those whose participation is absolutely necessary should be invited. These include:

- Those who are directly affected by the decision made at the meeting.
- Those with the specific knowledge.
- Those who are making the decisions.
- Those who have experience with similar problems.
- Those with administrative and legal responsibilities (e.g., the controller).
- Those respected as advisors and problem solvers or conference leaders.

6. Choose a suitable time for the meeting (participants should be available and have time to prepare).
7. Choose a suitable room where you won't be interrupted. Have any necessary visual aids available (overhead projector, flipcharts, etc.).

8. Set goals for the agenda, i.e., make clear what should be achieved by the meeting:

   • Decision (D)
   • Preparation of a decision (PD)
   • Problem solving (PS)
   • Information (I)

9. Set up an agenda with time estimates for each topic according to its importance or priority. Use the Business Meeting Checklist form on page 167 for that purpose.
10. Send out invitations or memos at least one week ahead accompanied by detailed information on topics and goals to be covered. (If possible, give the exact time for each topic if some participants will only come for certain topics.)

2. During the Meeting

11. Start on time. If you wait once for tardy participants, you'll always wait.
12. Announce the per minute costs for this meeting (salaries per minute plus 77.5 percent fringe benefits) and your intention to make this an efficient meeting. Be convincing in stating that the meeting will be successful.
13. Establish rules of cooperation (instead of standing orders), for example, an agreement limiting each contributor to the discussion to 30 or 60 seconds, or passing resolutions only with the consent of all participants.
14. Put one participant in charge of keeping time and the minutes.
15. Try to control interruptions and to block such "killer phrases" as "We never did it that way!" (See also the list of types of participants at meetings on page 169.)
16. Try to recognize critical points and occurrences during the discussion, such as distracting conversations, digressions, differences of opinion, an impasse, hasty or wrong decisions.

	Business Meeting Checklist

Subject/Theme _____

Date	DataBank #
Start	Finish

	Agenda	OK	Participants	OK
1				
2				
3				
4				
5				
6				
7				
8				
9				
10				

Subject

Decisions/Conclusions	Accountable

17. During the meeting make sure that its goals are being achieved through an analysis of the problem, alternative solutions, the decision-making process, information, and coordination.
18. Repeat the decisions achieved so as to ensure the participants' consent and to rule out misunderstandings.
19. At the end of the meeting, summarize the results and explain what has to be done, by whom, and by when.
20. Close the meeting on time. You'll gain the reputation of a good conference chairperson. At future meetings the participants will be disciplined just enough by themselves to finish the agenda in time. Nobody wants to be under the pressure of deadlines caused by meetings that run over. If you've set priorities on your agenda, make sure that the most important points were discussed at the beginning and that only unimportant things remain unfinished. Conclude the meeting in a positive way with a few friendly and personal remarks.

3.   After the Meeting

21. From time to time examine the course and outcome of the meeting by questioning the participants:

Types of Participants at Meetings

At meetings you will often encounter the same types of participants. Here are some suggestions on how to deal with them.

1. *The fighter.*   Stay calm and matter-of-fact. Induce the group to counter his or her arguments.
2. *The positive person.*   Let him or her summarize the results, and consciously involve this individual in the discussion.
3. *The know-it-all.*   Invite the group to comment on his or her arguments and assertions.
4. *The talkative person.*   Interrupt him or her with tact. Limit the time for talking.
5. *The shy person.*   Ask him or her easy, direct questions. Reinforce this person's confidence.
6. *The negative person.*   Acknowledge his or her knowledge and experience.
7. *The disinterested person.*   Ask about his or her work. Give examples from this person's area of expertise.
8. *The big shot.*   Don't criticize directly. Use the "yes, but . . ." method.
9. *The inquisitive person.*   Turn his or her questions back to the group.

- Were the causes and objectives of the meeting understood?
- Did everyone receive the agenda and additional information material in time before the meeting?
- Did the meeting start on time?
- Did everyone keep to the agenda?
- Did we achieve the goal of the meeting?
- Were tasks distributed and deadlines set?
- In terms of the whole meeting how much time was spent inefficiently?

22. Prepare minutes that clearly summarize the meeting. They should be produced and distributed within 24 or 48 hours at most. You will find an example on the following page. "The worst mistake after meetings is

having no minutes, the second worst is having bad minutes."

23. "Instant minutes" should be photocopied and handed out to the participants right after the meeting. In most cases a more elaborate version will be unnecessary. You'll find an example on p. 171.

24. Check to see if the steps decided upon were actually taken by the responsible party.

25. Unfinished tasks and problems should be the first points on the next agenda.

6.4   EFFICIENT ONE-ON-ONE CONVER-SATIONS—HOW TO MANAGE VISITORS

Visitors constitute a problem for managers in many ways. Receiving visitors often takes up more time than any other activity. A Swedish study has shown that, on average, managers spend as much as three and a half hours per day with visitors (mostly with staff members).

How high is your average? _____ hrs. (Check your Analysis of time and Activities form in the Introduction.)

The inability to predict whether a visitor has important information leads to many, often superfluous one-on-one conversations. This is a purely factual comment. From a socio-psychological perspective many visitor problems stem from our desire for contacts and for establishing social relationships. The worst time wasters are sudden, unannounced visitors you agree to see because you are afraid of missing out on something by not listening to them.

Reasons for visiting emerge from one or several of the following issues:

- Seeking information.
- Seeking help or advice.
- Giving out information.
- Responding to your invitation or casual remark. ("Why don't you drop by if you're in the neighborhood?")
- Maintaining social or friendly relationships.

Dept.:	Meeting Minutes		Date:
Topic:		Place:	
		Date:	
		From-to:	
Chairperson:	Responsible for Minutes: Tel.:	Invite/Agenda Date:	
Participants (Recipients of Minutes)		Other Recipients of Minutes	
Results		Suggestion Deadline	Control
No.	Can be continued on additional pages		Page:

The last issue can easily get out of hand (in terms of time), since many visitors drop by "just to say hello." In most cases these visitors don't want advice, but reassurance and support for their plans. The first strategy of visitor management is, therefore, to screen out unnecessary and unplanned visitors. The following discussion will focus on how to deal with visitors and will provide 10 suggestions on how to end a conversation.

Strategies of Visitor Management

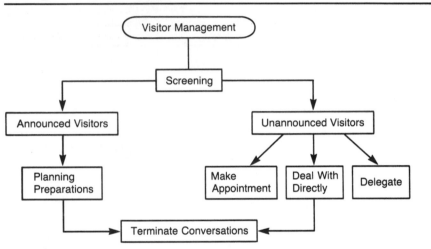

1. Screening of Visitors

It's especially important for managers to have uninterrupted time for thinking and working. Protect yourself against unwanted interruptions by visitors, at least for a certain time during the day. This applies also—or especially—to your staff. Having a staff-oriented management style is often misinterpreted as implying that a staff member should have access to his or her boss at any time. It is a time-wasting luxury if a manager is available any day of the week and at any time during the day either in person or by phone. In such a case visitors will often come to your office without a reason.

Protect yourself against these visitors with the following 12-point program:

1. Make your secretary responsible for your appointments. Appointments should be made ahead of time.
2. Make your secretary's desk into a barrier that no one can pass without being seen and asked, "What can I do for you?" or "Can he or she call you back?"
3. Initiate a quiet hour, for example, at the beginning of your workday during which you cannot be reached.
4. Establish general visitation or office hours, and have your secretary ask the reason for a visit so that you can be prepared.
5. Have regular office hours for meeting with your staff (e.g., Smith, Thursdays, 2 to 3 P.M.).
6. Go to your staff's offices and be open for questions. It is much easier to say good-bye and leave a room than to usher someone out of your office.
7. Receive visitors standing, for example, in the anteroom; during the welcoming you can decide about the priority or necessity of this visit. Once your conversation partner sits down you're (from a psychological perspective) at a disadvantage.
8. Try to come earlier to the office rather than staying late.
9. Isolate yourself, for example, in a separate office or someone else's office; only your secretary should know about it.
10. Attend to your personal relationships at another time—not in your office. You can make regular appointments to meet important people for lunch and so forth.
11. Place your desk out of sight of the open door in order not to encourage potential visitors.

12. And most of all: put an end to the myth of the open door (management by open doors).

Leave your office door open if you want to be reached; close it if you don't want to be disturbed.

2. Planning and Preparing for Unannounced Visitors

Every visitor thinks he or she has an important reason to seek a conversation.

1. For each visitor ask what purpose this conversation should serve.
2. At the beginning of his or her visit discuss the goals of your conversation.
3. Right away set a time limit for the conversation; this is because a conversation will take as long as there is time. Note the time in your daily planner.
4. If necessary, postpone a planned topic or the whole conversation if you can't reach your goal within the time limit.
5. You should exchange information of a private nature at the end of your conversation after you've finished the warming-up phase.
6. Let your secretary watch the time during the visit; arrange for her to remind you of it or to intervene saying, "You'll have to leave for XYZ in half an hour."
7. Try to prepare the contents of your conversation (background of the problem, earlier discussions and decisions), at least briefly, and have the necessary material at hand.
8. Be prepared for any arguments and objections that your visitor may have.
9. Make sure that this conversation is really necessary, and see if there aren't any alternatives, for example, a telephone call or a work lunch.
10. Prepare for the conversation by using a Dialog Preparation form like the one shown on page 175.

Dialog Preparations

My Goals

Necessary Documents

Dialog Opening

What Could Be the
Client's Bottleneck?

My Suggestion

Expected Objections

My Counter-Arguments

My Strengths

Notes/Analysis/Evaluation

To Be Arranged Immediately:

You must consider the following factors in preparing your conversation:

Planning:

- Appointment
- Topic
- Time limit
- Preparation
- Documents

Opening:

- Short welcome
- Tackle the problem immediately

Course of conversation:

- Stay with the topic
- Listen actively

Closing:

- Task distribution (follow-up)
- Keep within time limit
- Short summary
- Close with friendly remarks

Conversations with Your Staff.   Because of your working relationship, visits from your staff members can be better controlled and fitted into your time plan than visits by colleagues from other departments:

- Set up regular office hours for your staff in which you can discuss the problems that have accumulated in the meantime.
- Reserve a page in your time planner for each member of your staff.
- Have short staff meetings on a regular basis to deal with simple work or administrative problems.
- Once in a while have lunch with members of your staff to tend to the need for personal contact.
- Make your staff write a short note or call you if there is no need for a face-to-face talk.

3. How to Deal with Unannounced Visitors

The way you will deal with unannounced visitors will largely depend on whether you have enough time to talk, whether your visitor comes to you with justifiable requests, and what experience you had with him or her in earlier conversations.

You should begin by asking about the purpose of the visit (What? Who? Why? How? With what? When). Depending on the response you receive to this inquiry, you should delegate the visit to a staff member or a different department or go ahead with the conversation if you can deal with it in a short period of time. In this way, you limit the extent of the interruption. In other cases, make an appointment and dismiss the visitor.

The best method is to accustom your visitors to regular office hours and hours during which you don't want to be disturbed.

4. How to End a Conversation

All conversations must come to an end, whether they are productive or unproductive. Even if you waste only five minutes a visit and have only five visitors a day, you'll still lose more than two hours per week. If your visitor doesn't want to end the conversation, try the following polite or—depending on the situation—not so polite methods:

1. Make summarizing or concluding remarks.
2. Bring the professional part of your conversation to an end by starting to chat about other things.
3. Take a look at your watch or have some sort of signal go off after a given interval.
4. Look bored.
5. Get up.
6. Lead your visitor to the door.
7. Start reading your mail while your visitor is still speaking.
8. Have your secretary interrupt you and remind you of your next appointment.

9. Start talking more forcefully and quickly.
10. Inform your visitor at the beginning and toward the end of your discussion that you're expecting another visitor and that your time is limited.

Finally, you may have to simply say that you would like to end this conversation.

6.5   HOW TO BE EFFICIENT ON THE PHONE

The telephone is the most widely used but also the most stressful means of communication; and therefore, it is the most frequent source of interruption in the business world. Nine out of 10 managers spend at least an hour per day on the phone, four out of 10 spend more than two hours.

You can't live with the phone and you can't live without it. Aren't we all only too familiar with the almighty ringing of the telephone? How many managers on their way out the door will go back to their desk because the phone is ringing? How many housewives (or husbands) will interrupt dinner preparations, just because the phone is ringing? How about you?

Aside from the time-efficiency perspective, a telephone call is somewhat like an unwanted house call whereby someone intrudes upon you. A lot of people wouldn't dare to enter your office without being announced. But with a telephone they can do so at any time, protected by their geographical and personal distance. Once a connection is established, it can easily lead to unnecessary time-wasting conversations.

Nowadays a lot of jobs are essentially telephone jobs, such as that of a stockbroker, investment adviser, or supplier of information services. You can even get advice and therapy over the phone. Using the phone becomes easier and more convenient all the time. But the increasing use of the phone as a means of communication may cause us to make a lot of costly mistakes.

Ten Telephone Sins
1. You're unclear about your objective.
2. You're insufficiently prepared.

3. You call at a bad time.
4. You have to search for the number.
5. You don't have the necessary documents at hand.
6. You haven't made any preliminary notes.
7. You don't state your purpose clearly.
8. You hold a monologue instead of listening and asking questions.
9. You don't take any notes.
10. You don't come to any definite agreement.

A lot of people make telephone calls because they're looking for advice, in need of contact or admiration, want to appear busy or important, just want to let off steam, or want to chat because they're bored. How about you?

Telephone calls should be primarily used as a means of efficient communication. If we use the phone properly, it can save us a lot of time. At the same time it is the most common source of interruption. So we have to confront the paradox of the telephone: It's both a great way to save time and one of the most common time wasters. Whether you save or waste time on the phone depends on (1) how sensibly you use it, and (2) how willing you are to rid yourself of bad telephone habits.

Here is some advice that may help you become more efficient on the telephone. We need first to differentiate between (1) passive phone calls (that is, how to deal with incoming calls) and (2) active phone calls (that is, how to prepare for outgoing calls—calls you yourself make).

1. The Telephone as a Means to Better Organization

The telephone has five advantages over written means of telecommunication such as the telegram, telex, fax machine, and especially over the letter:

- The Speed of Transmission (Advantage of Time). The connection between communicators can be established immediately, provided the other party can be reached. It is possible to obtain necessary information while working, and there is no need to postpone activities.

Strategies for Efficient Phone Calls

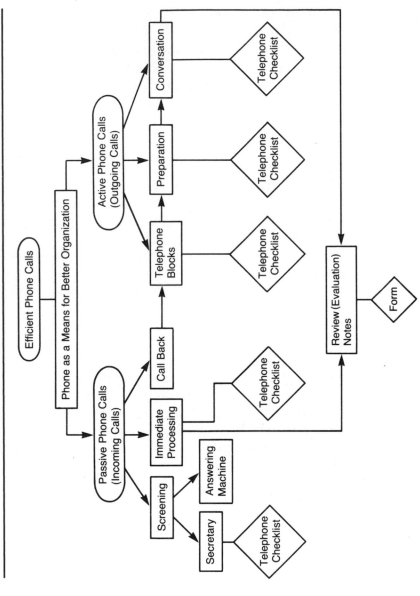

- The Direct/Immediate Exchange of Information (Advantage of Dialogue).   Questions can be solved immediately as a result of feedback, and agreements made because of the direct contact between sender and receiver.
- The Advantage of Personal Contact.   While a letter is often reserved and factual, in a phone conversation you can be more friendly, personal, and lively. If you want to get something from your conversation partner, you're in a stronger position on the phone. There you can refute reservations and objections, whereas in a written communication a negative reply may have already arrived. You can solve misunderstandings immediately. For example, sales over the phone are much more successful than advertisements or advertising letters.
- No Paperwork (Advantage of Simplicity).   All activities connected with writing (dictating, typing, reading, editing, signing, sending off) are avoided.
- Money Savings (Advantage of Low Costs).   Based on the calculation that a letter will cost from $10 to $20 in administrative costs, even a long-distance call that lasts three to five minutes is cheaper. You can save trips that otherwise would be made just for the purpose of personal contact. Meetings of two or more people can be replaced by conference calls, and you can thus save travel time and expense.

Furthermore, difficult problems can be solved more easily and faster by a phone call than by a letter. The advantages of a telephone conversation over a letter are especially pronounced in complex cases. Therefore, don't dictate—use the phone.

Now let's consider passive phone calls (incoming calls). To ensure an uninterrupted, goal-oriented working environment, managers should prevent incoming phone calls (like other sources of interruption) from disrupting their concentration on important tasks. You can prevent this by screening your calls.

2. Screening

Everyone calling you is convinced that his or her purpose is important. Therefore, you'll have to treat every caller as important. On the other hand, if you want anything else done within an eight- or nine-hour day, you don't have enough time to do so. Unfortunately, rejecting a phone call you've agreed to is (apart from dismissing a visitor) one of the most difficult interpersonal tasks. And you can hardly predict what consequences your rejection will have.

Therefore, it is better and more effective if you have unnecessary phone calls screened or transferred to another time that is more convenient for you:

- Inform all potential regular callers (staff members, colleagues, clients, friends, etc.) about when you can't be reached.
- Try to arrange for daily telephone hours when you can deal with requests in one block.
- Don't forget to tell potential callers the best time to reach you.
- At the end of a phone conversation try to avoid the phrase "Why don't you call me again!" Only say it if you really mean it.
- Don't let others wait for information from you. Call promptly (at a time convenient for you), before they call you.
- If possible, let your secretary accept all incoming calls or use at times an answering machine.

a. Screening by a Secretary. A secretary accepting, screening, and transferring calls based on a priority system is the biggest key to a manager's effectiveness. Analyses have shown that a great number of incoming phone calls need to be redirected. Other staff members or departments can often supply the requested information better and faster. Here is some practical advice:

- Your secretary should always request the purpose of the call so as to be able to judge how pressing or important

it is. Every caller with a really important request will be understanding if asked politely.
• Supply your secretary with a checklist of criteria that will tell her or him when to reject, postpone, or put through a call.

Secretary's Telephone Checklist
1. What is the purpose of the call?
2. Which calls should be transferred immediately to someone in your staff or another department?
3. What topics should be dealt with by your secretary?
4. At what times are you generally not available (quiet or phoneless hour)?
5. For whom are you not available (maybe through a letter)?
6. For whom are you available only at certain times (phone hour, office hour)?
7. For whom are you available at all times?
8. When should private calls be put through? Who?
9. When is it most convenient for you to call back?
10. When is it convenient for the caller to be called back?

Never have your calls screened by having your secretary say:

". . . is in an important meeting."
". . . doesn't want to be disturbed."   ·
". . . has an important visitor."

These or similar phrases easily produce an uneasy feeling on the part of the caller who wants to be taken seriously; on a social level this message says "The other person is more important than you" (otherwise he or she would talk to you now). A caller should not feel neglected or turned away. You don't have to tell callers what you're doing, either.

An example of a neutral expression would be: "Mr. X is not in right now (at lunch), he's expected back by 2:00 P.M. Can we call you back?" If your secretary isn't sure whether to put a call through, she or he can make the caller decide on the relative importance or urgency of the call by saying "Ms. Y is in an important meeting right now—shall I interrupt her?" In most cases this strategy will work well since the caller understands that his or her call is not being ignored or neglected.

   b.   Screening by an Answering Machine. If, for some period of time you don't have a secretary, you can temporarily use an answering machine as an automatic screening device for incoming calls. While a number of people have reservations about an answering machine, its advantage over not answering the phone at all is that you can listen to the messages and interrupt or call back later.

3.   Immediate Processing

In exceptional cases, when important calls have to be put through and during your telephone hours, you should begin by clarifying a few points that will make immediate processing of phone calls more efficient. Have a note-pad at hand.

   Telephone Checklist for Immediate Processing
   1. Who exactly is the caller, from which company, in what function, etc.?
   2. What is the purpose of the call?
   3. How urgent and important is this?
   4. When can you call back?
   5. Where can you reach the caller? (If this is the first contact, get the address, phone and telex number, spelling of name.)

   Another way of dealing immediately with a call is to have the secretary ask the caller to hold on for a moment while saying, "I'll see if I can disturb him (or her)." The secretary will then ask you for a short answer, which in most cases will satisfy the caller. This is a fast and easy way of dealing with this interruption, and the manager's work is barely disrupted (no greeting or saying good-bye to the caller, no long discussions).

At the same time you have complied with the importance of the call.

If you can be reached by phone directly or you don't have a secretary or answering machine, fend off unnecessary calls by saying, "I'll call you back" or "Please, call back at 4:00 P.M." Otherwise, follow the checklist.

4. Calling Back

Calling back is another efficient method of dealing with incoming calls. Even if you call back at a time that is not as convenient to the original caller, it is an effective means of self-management: Why should his or her reason for calling be more important than your wanting to continue your work?

A successful manager once said about calling back, "No one expects a doctor or surgeon to interrupt an examination or surgery to answer the phone. No one expects an attorney to answer the phone during a trial. No one expects a professor to go to the phone during a lecture. Why should it be expected that a business man is always there, when the telephone rings?"[2]

Calling back in blocks of telephone time greatly reduces the number of interruptions and produces a lot of advantages in terms of saving and systematizing your time. This method allows the secretary to gather the necessary documents for the manager, which again reduces the actual time on the phone. Before returning calls, you have gained time to think about your answer if the caller has mentioned the purpose for the phone inquiry.

Active Phone Calls (Outgoing Calls). It is easier to make a phone call than to handle incoming calls since you can control the former. The most effective method is to make phone calls in blocks of telephone time.

---

[2]Joseph M. Trickett, "A More Effective Use of Time," *California Management Review,* Summer 1962).

5. Blocks of Telephone Time

Choose two periods, for example, one late in the morning and one in the afternoon, during which you can deal with all your phone calls. The advantages of grouping together smaller, similar tasks are that you only have to prepare once for this activity, and you stay with tasks of a similar kind. Experiment with ways of working most effectively with this method. Keep in mind, though, that a block of telephone time shouldn't last much longer than 30 minutes; otherwise, your constantly busy line will annoy callers.

Using this method you won't be making phone calls at random but purposefully and more effectively. Your concentration will be higher and you won't be disturbed by incoming calls (since you're blocking your own line). If you establish the goal of your conversation beforehand, you will only raise important matters. You won't waste time during the conversation, hastily searching for documents since you've organized everything in advance.

If you deal with all your phone calls consecutively and within a certain period of time, you will handle them more effectively and automatically force yourself to limit the time that you're on the phone (self-discipline). You can also expand this principle to half a day or even a whole day, and use this telephone day to deal with all the activities on your weekly plan that can be handled over the phone.

We recommend the following procedures:

- Make a list of all the names, phone numbers, and topics, and then organize them according to priority according to a priority code (e.g., A, B, C, or 1, 2, 3). (See the Eisenhower principle in Chapter 3.4.)
- If possible, try to refrain from making less important and less pressing calls.
- Check your list for possibilities to delegate and assign the respective calls to your secretary or staff.
- Organize all necessary documents and files to correspond with the order of your phone calls.
- You may want to start a file called *phone calls*.

- Start processing your first block of telephone calls; your secretary should dial the numbers according to your list until you reach someone you want to talk to. Calls that cannot be completed automatically move to the end of the waiting list and then are dialed again. After two or three unsuccessful attempts to reach the other party, move the call to the afternoon block of telephone calls.
- Let your secretary dial the number and take the call only when the connection is established (this refers to single phone calls, too).

In the long run you will save a lot of time this way.

Using Your Time Planner. In briefly preparing one or several calls, use the left side of your daily plan (backside of the previous day). Write down any questions and actions taken.

Telephone List/Directory   **Date:** _____

Call No.	Name	Topic	Phone No.	Priority	Control

Further Possibilities. Here are some additional suggestions:

- Routine phone calls should be dealt with as a block during an unproductive period when they won't interfere with the rest of your work.
- Use waiting periods or other moments between tasks or meetings to return a few calls.
- Use your phone countercyclically, that is, not within peak hours. You'll be able to reach the other party much faster. The most desirable hours are:
    8:00 A.M.–9:30A.M.
    1:30 P.M.–2:00 P.M.
    after 4:30 P.M.

During other hours of the day you'll probably need double the amount of time for your calls, and the other party will be immediately available probably only 50 percent of the time.

6. Preparations

Before you make a call, ask the following basic questions:

- Is personal contact absolutely necessary?
- In order to reach an agreement, is it absolutely necessary to know the answer?
- Am I going to see the other party in the near future?

Not making a call can be better than calling without a goal or without results. You should only call when you are aware of your objectives:

- Do I just want to get in contact with somebody and exchange thoughts?
- Do I want to become reacquainted, or do I want to start a new relationship?
- Do I want to receive or provide information?
- Do I want to present ideas and have them evaluated?
- Do I want to convince the other party of my intentions and explain my ideas?

Try to find the right time for your conversation:

- Try to find out when is the best time to call. The person you call will be thankful—just like you—if his or her work is interrupted as little as possible. You can find out about it at the end of another phone call or a personal conversation.
- Announce your call beforehand. The other party will be prepared and available if you announce the exact time in advance (by letter, telex, or your secretary). You'll save time and money and expedite the process.

Prepare your calls in terms of facts and context. Getting ready for your conversation is very important. The following checklist will provide you with suggestions on how to use this tool more effectively. Prepare yourself for the other party and then concentrate on the conversation. Prepare first—call later!

Checklist of Telephone Preparations
Goals

1. What do I want to achieve?
2. Whom do I want to call? (name, extension, department, position)
3. When do I want to call? (Consider the lunch hour, flexible work hours, office hours, etc.)
4. What questions do I have? (Write down the key words.)

Documents

5. What documents do I need? (correspondence, customer files, reports)
6. What documents does the other party need?

Arguments and Objections

7. What is the other party's goal?
8. How can I motivate him or her? (Do I know the impact of my activity on him/her?)
9. How should I present my arguments?
10. What evidence, references, or examples could I use?
11. What questions should I expect from him or her?
12. What objections should I expect?
13. How do I refute these objections?
14. What should I not say?
15. What will the other party conceal from me?
16. How do I get to this information?
17. What compromises or concessions could I make?
18. How can we finish in such a way that everybody wins?

Results

19. What did I achieve?
20. What do I have to arrange?
    Who will do it?
    When?
    Where?

7. The Conversation

There is no reason for us to give elaborate advice here on such obvious technical details as the need to pronounce your words clearly, to keep the mouthpiece free of any obstructions, to identify yourself by giving your name and then to repeat it, if necessary. You should keep in mind the strategic considerations given in the above checklist, especially in the section entitled "arguments and objections." Here are a few additional suggestions for your conversation after you've reached the other party.

    1. Make it brief. The opening phase of a telephone conversation will determine both its course and its conclusion. "Hello, John, how are you doing?" might trigger a long conversation on family issues, vacation, hobbies, and current events. Don't exchange weather reports; just keep it brief!

    "Hello, John! I just need some information, if you can spare a minute" or similar phrases are not impolite, but they may guarantee a short conversation and make it easier for the other party to be efficient, too. If personal contact is essential to achieve your goal, you can briefly talk about a shared experience. In calling strangers it is appropriate to briefly introduce yourself to create a positive atmosphere.

    2. Inform the other party what the call is all about, and then go into any necessary details.

    3. Don't stop a conversation when an important call comes in on the other line. In an emergency, ask if you can interrupt the conversation, and then assure the other party that you'll call back in 10 minutes.

    4. Avoid talking to people in your office while you're on the phone.

    5. Request the other party's approval if you're taping the conversation or letting others listen in.

    6. At the end of a long conversation, briefly summarize the results and steps that have to be taken (Who does what when?).

7. Request or promise a short written confirmation of your agreement. The easiest way is to copy your notes of the conversation and sign them.

8. During the conversation write down important details, such as names, figures, and essential information. (Make it legible so that it can be read and understood by your staff, too.)

9. Monitor the time of your conversation, especially for long-distance calls.

10. Make it brief. End the conversation as soon as you've reached your goal. Many phone conversations take forever because both parties have trouble coming to a conclusion. "Thanks very much, John. I think that's all. Hope to see you again soon!" is efficient and polite, and personal. Try to get your conversational partners used to your brief but polite style on the phone. Keep in mind that the last impression should be the best.

The following list summarizes the most important points:

Make It Brief
1. Keep the opening phase to a minimum.
2. First say what the call is all about.
3. Don't stop because of other incoming calls.
4. Avoid talking to a third party.
5. Get prior approval for taping or having others listen in on the conversation.
6. Summarize the results and any additional steps that are needed.
7. Ask for written confirmation of any agreements.
8. Write down important details.
9. Monitor the time and the cost of the conversation.
10. Discontinue the conversation when you've reached your goal.

Analysis of the Conversation. The last step in a telephone conversation is documenting what took place. Since phone calls are the most frequent source of misunderstandings, you should get used to making notes of all important calls. In this way you'll document all the information obtained and have valuable proof of what took place if you need it later. You can write on the document you referred to during the conversation—such as a letter you had at hand—or on a separate sheet. Stationery stores offer a variety of forms such as the one shown below:

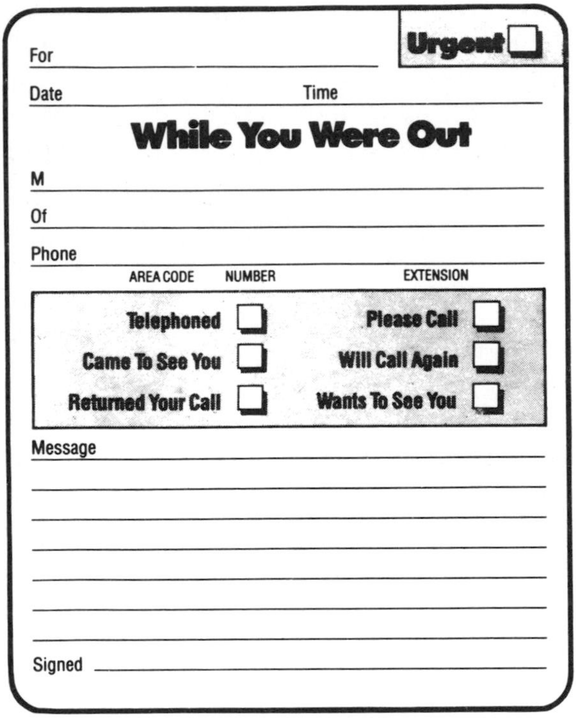

For		Urgent ☐
Date		Time

While You Were Out

M _____

Of _____

Phone _____

AREA CODE   NUMBER   EXTENSION

Telephoned ☐	Please Call ☐
Came To See You ☐	Will Call Again ☐
Returned Your Call ☐	Wants To See You ☐

Message _____

Signed _____

Here again we'd like to suggest that you develop your own forms. The following example can assist you in preparing for your call, noting information obtained, and analyzing the call.

Telephone Notes   Date _____

Who?		Where?
What?		
Before	During	After

6.6 EFFICIENT CORRESPONDENCE

Dealing inefficiently with correspondence can lead to an enormous waste of time. Often managers are busy processing their unavoidable correspondence for more than an hour a day. While processing incoming mail, writing routine and individual letters, and dictating, time losses accumulate that could have been avoided with more systematic work methods. The following suggestions should motivate you to deal more economically with C or B tasks.

1. Efficiently Processing Incoming Mail

1. Look only at the incoming mail of importance to you, not at the routine mail.
2. Have all incoming mail presorted (e.g., according to priorities) and presented to you in a folder.
3. Have existing files (for each case) added to the incoming letters so that you can refer to them.
4. Everything that has no informational value or doesn't have to be processed or kept should go into the wastebasket.
5. As you read a letter, immediately mark all important passages so as to make any later processing easier.

6. Immediately mark a letter with standard processing symbols; for example, use key words to indicate the deadlines for a reply, who is to process the letter, who is to distribute it, and where to file it.
7. Immediately transfer incoming mail that should be processed at another office.
8. If possible, deal with an incoming letter almost immediately, i.e., while checking your mail (see below).
9. Try not to process any document (e.g., read it) without doing something about it or setting in motion some action on it. Your goal should be to process each document only once!
10. Get a desk organizer for your mail with three sections for:
    Immediate processing
    Reviewing
    Filing

2.   Efficiently Processing Outgoing Mail

Whether you're writing routine or personalized letters, you should always work according to the following principle: only write or dictate as much as absolutely necessary! The following suggestions may save you only a few minutes, but over several months, it will add up to hours.

1. Immediate Replies.   Write an answer on the original incoming letter, add the date and your signature, and send it back to the sender (keep a copy for your records). Often remarks such as "I agree" or "OK" will be a sufficient answer. You can reinforce the positive effect of this time-saving method by using a sticker or stamp:

(Company Name)

Immediate/Quick Reply: Fast + Effective

The advantages of this method are:

- You're saving time otherwise needed to dictate or write a reply.
- You're answering by return mail.
- You're saving 50 percent of paperwork on both sides (two processes = one letter).

2. *Letter Copies.* Here is a variation of the quick-reply method: If you have a question concerning a certain document or want to order something out of a catalogue, advertisement, or article, put your card or address label onto the original and make a copy of both. Write your question, order, etc. onto the copy and send it to the addressee.

The advantages of this method are:

- You don't have to draft a letter and have it typed up.
- The addressee knows right away what you want as you are sending back his or her original communication.

3. *Redi-Letters.* This method is helpful if your message requires an answer and the texts involved are short.

Send the original to the addressee (with a copy for your files). After you've received the answer you can destroy the copy. The advantages of this method are:

- The limited space for the message and the answer will ensure a brief correspondence.
- The addressee and sender have both the message and the answer in front of them at the same time.
- Both have only one piece of correspondence to file.
- There's no need to duplicate.

4. *Answering Letters.* Here is a way to show consideration for the business executive with whom you are corresponding. Just as you expect a short, quick answer to your communication, you can save your business correspondent some time if you:

- Send a sheet along with your letter stating, for example, "Please use the attached sheet for a short, handwritten reply."

---

redi-letter   **carbonless**   806924   TRIP

TO

F
R
O
M

| SUBJECT | DATE / / |

MESSAGE

SIGNED

REPLY

SIGNED   DATE / /

SEND PARTS 1 AND 3 INTACT -
PART 3 WILL BE RETURNED WITH REPLY.   *carbonless*

- Leave room for an answer with the remark: "My answer is. . . . ."
- Encourage short replies by adding that it's OK to send a brief reply.
- Coordinate these methods with your business correspondents, for example, by mentioning in conversations that long letters are not necessary and that you want to make it easier for them to reply.

5. Communication Forms. Use forms or form letters for short messages, orders, memos, etc., if you want to communicate short, standardized messages or send documents that need only a minimal explanation. Stationery stores offer a wide variety of such forms.

RAPID
MEMO

TO: _____

DATE: _____
SUBJECT: _____

AVOID VERBAL ORDERS

"SAY IT IN WRITING"

DATE: NO.:

TO:

SIGNED:

NOTICE—Keep This For Reference

The advantages of standardized forms are that you can save time when you only have to check off an instruction or write a few words. Processing mail at once will often make a better impression than nice, long, but ineffective letters.

6. Word Processing. A boom in microelectronics, along with falling prices for personal computers, has made the use of word processing in business increasingly attractive. One advantage is that programmed letters save a lot of time while still maintaining the appeal of personal letters.

7. Individual Letters. Finally, there are a lot of cases where you'll still have to write a personalized letter. We suggest that you:

- Accumulate single letters in a correspondence folder so that you can handle them all together on a mass-production basis.
- Have all necessary documents, notes, etc. at hand as you prepare your correspondence.
- Use short drafts focusing on the main points so that you can fully concentrate on the proper phrasing.
- Use a dictaphone for simple letters or, even better, you might delegate more by giving your secretary only a rough outline using key words (e.g., cancel appointment). See also the suggestions for how to process incoming mail given earlier in this chapter.
- Finally, consider whether you can't address the issue over the phone. Very often you can clarify several points at once, and a call takes less time than dictating a letter.

8. Efficient Dictating. We assume that you're familiar with the common techniques of efficient dictating so we will only add a few suggestions:

- While waiting in a car, train, or plane, use your dictaphone for short dictations.
- Check to see if you can give your secretary just a rough outline (key words) from which she or he can compare the whole text of a letter.
- Group together short dictating tasks, especially those dealing with less important matters.

9. Goal-Oriented Approach to Your Work. Before dictating or writing a letter ask yourself what you want to achieve. Decide what you want to communicate ahead of time.

6.7 STREAMLINING YOUR WORK WITH CHECKLISTS AND STANDARDIZED FORMS

By using checklists to systematize recurring tasks, you'll save additional time. The term *checklist* was originally used by pilots to describe a precise listing of what has to be done, checked, or changed. Today checklists have evolved into a universal instrument for addressing recurring or similar tasks in the business world. They have the following advantages:

1. By breaking a task down into individual phases you can concentrate more on important issues.
2. By processing a task more quickly, you can unleash extra energy.
3. Routine tasks don't have to be thought through again and again.
4. You don't have to worry about forgetting anything. Checklists offer maximum security with minimum control.
5. Checklists serve as starting points for future experiences and improvements.
6. By breaking tasks down into single steps, you are able to clarify any unclear activities.
7. Checklists are tools to help you prepare for work assignments.
8. Checklists offer a basic structure that can be changed or improved upon again and again.
9. By automatizing the way you process recurring or similar tasks, checklists produce a sense of achievement.
10. Checklists are based on experience and do not require you to use a lot of thinking power on less important tasks.

When should you use checklists? First, they can serve as an instrument or tool to guide the ways in which you obtain information, form an opinion, or reach a decision. Second, checklists are appropriate means by which you can analyze a situation, record your observations, exercise controls, carry on negotiations and discussions, hold talks, or plan a trip. There are a very few meaningful activities that cannot be broken down into separate phases.

Look for recurring activities at the office or at home, and then make up your own checklists for such activities as the following:

• Travel preparations
• Preparing for meetings (see the Business Meeting Checklist on page 167)

- Dictating
- Controlling projects (see the Project Management Check-list on page 99)
- Analyzing problems
- Acting as a troubleshooter for your car

Use the space below to note some ideas you might use later in developing your own checklists.

1.
2.
3.
4.
5.

The basic structure of a checklist can be developed in the following way:

Five Steps in Developing a Checklist
1. Pick a task or activity:
   That is recurring.
   That is processed similarly.
2. Break down procedure into individual work phases:
   What has to be done?
   What do I have to consider?
   Who has to be asked or contacted?
   Whom do I have to inform?
3. Build a logical sequence:
   What are the interdependencies?
   What time-related conditions have to be kept?
   What is logically based on what?
   Where are interim results needed?
4. Build groups of tasks:
   What activities are repetitive?
   Where are logical break points?
5. Review a temporary checklist with the following aims in mind:
   To analyze mistakes.
   To pinpoint critical phases.
   To find possibilities for delegation.

To have a trial run.
To produce a finished checklist.

Make up a list of your recurring tasks and try to develop checklists according to the five-step method.

Recurring Tasks

1.
2.
3.
4.
5.
6.
7.
8.
9.
10.

Try to determine how much time and work you can save in terms of minutes and tasks. You can save even more time by using checklists or similar forms for projects and processes.

- You can find an example of a Project Management checklist on page 99.
- An example of a Prospective Customers/Acquisition checklist can be found on page 202.
- Develop your own forms.
- Review forms already in use in terms of their structure, purpose, and completeness.

6.8   SUMMARY AND ANALYSIS

- Communication is the exchange of information. In processing information, always remember your personal or career goals.
- The first component of efficient reading involves selecting the material and then deciding what and how much is to be read (setting priorities).
- You can also improve your reading speed (words per minute) through special training:

Prospective Customers Acquisition Checklist			

Client

Contact Person	Position
Address	City/State/Zip
Phone #	Branch of Industry

	Visit	☎	✉

Decision to Buy Is Influenced by:

Name	Position
Name	Position

Motivation to Buy Is Influenced by:	Strongly	Somewhat	Little
Price/Price Level			
Quality of Product/Productivity			
Delivery-Service			
Availability/Date of Delivery			
Customer Service			

Notes:

To Be Arranged Immediately:

To reduce bad habits and interruptions.
To use better reading techniques.
- By marking important passages and making excerpts you'll also ensure:
Better processing of the reading material.
Easier rereading of the material by highlighting essential information.
- The SQ 3R method can be used as a summarizing reading technique to:
Survey
Question
Read
Recapitulate
Review
- The following checklist summarizes the most important suggestions and rules for efficient meetings:

Organizing Principles for Efficient Meetings
Before the Meeting

1. Is it necessary to meet at all?
2. What alternatives are there?
3. Do you really have to participate?
4. Attend only as long as necessary.
5. Keep the number of participants as small as possible.
6. Choose a suitable date and time for meeting.
7. Look for rooms where there will be no interruptions and supply visual aids.
8. Define goals for the agenda.
9. Note the approximate time for each item on the agenda.
10. Send out invitations that give information on topics and goals.

During the Meeting

11. Start on time.
12. Announce the per minute costs for this meeting.

13. Define rules for cooperation.
14. Appoint a person responsible for keeping time and minutes.
15. Eliminate interruptions and killer comments.
16. Watch out for critical points in the discussion.
17. Check the goals of the meeting.
18. Repeat the decisions and actions to be taken.
19. Summarize the results.
20. Finish on time and offer some positive or personal remarks.

After the Meeting

21. Check the course and success of the meeting.
22. Write a summary of the results.
23. Copy and distribute an abbreviated version of the minutes.
24. Check the plan for the next action steps.
25. Defer unfinished items to the next agenda.

- Try to screen unwanted visitors and dispense with the myth of management by open doors.
- Introduce quiet hours and office hours (even for your staff). Plan and prepare talks with announced visitors (purpose or goal, etc.).
- The telephone is an effective means for saving time, but also one of the most frequent time wasters (telephone paradox). Learn to manage your phone (self-management), instead of being managed by your phone.
- Prevent interruptions through screening (by your secretary) and use the call-back method to deal with incoming calls.
- Make outgoing calls in telephone blocks (morning or afternoon), and prepare the content of your calls (checklist).
- Keep your phone calls brief and make notes of your phone calls (before, during, and after the call).
- Reduce and systematize your correspondence:

Incoming Mail	Outgoing Mail
1. Don't deal with routine mail.	1. Immediate replies.
2. Sort mail in folders.	2. Letter copies.
3. Have documents attached.	3. Redi-letters.
4. Throw unimportant mail into the wastebasket.	4. Answering aids.
5. Mark important passages.	5. Short letters.
6. Add processing remarks.	6. Word processing.
7. Transfer mail to other offices, where appropriate.	7. Individual letters.
8. Process the mail immediately.	8. Dictating.
9. Leave no unprocessed documents.	9. Self-restrictions.
10. Provide your files with three sections.	10. Goal-oriented approach to work.

Checklists help you to concentrate on essential things and to save time for the following reasons:

1. You choose tasks or activities that can be streamlined in this way.
2. You break down a process into its separate stages.
3. You build a logical sequence.
4. You can group tasks together.
5. You can review the temporary checklist.

Forms similar to checklists (outlines, lists) can also help you to save time.

Now you can analyze Chapter 6 for your personal use.

- As I was reading this chapter, what seemed to be of special importance?
- What new insights did I gain?
- Were any assumptions of mine confirmed?
- What do I want to put into practice?

Analysis of Chapter 6

Result No.	Pages	Ideas, Suggestions, Topics of Value	Target Dates for Attainment	Control

Try to be more autonomous and shield yourself from visitors, phone calls, and meetings that will eat up your time. Uncontrolled and excessive communication is a key problem in achieving a personal work style; it is also the greatest time waster.

CHAPTER 7

TRANSFERRING: HOW TO PUT THEORY INTO PRACTICE

Everything is hard before it becomes easy.

Persian proverb

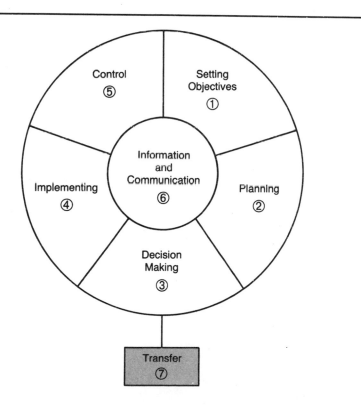

7.1 LOOKING BACKWARD AND FORWARD

Since you have now learned the functions and possibilities of self-management, this chapter can help you profitably analyze the experience you have gained and transfer the results into permanent practice.

At certain times you were probably thinking, "I would like to try this or that suggestion," for example, to set priorities (ABC), to buy a time planner, to make daily plans, to use the phone differently, etc.—and you may have entered these steps into the evaluation tables at the end of each chapter.

In this last chapter we will show you how to develop an overall strategic concept from the individual steps, and how to transfer this concept into your everyday activities. We suggest that you go through the individual chapters once again and enter all the suggestions you wanted to adopt into the Action Plan for Self-Management on this page. In doing so, you need to keep the following questions in mind:

1. What do you want to tackle?
2. Who will be affected by this action (you, your staff, your secretary, etc.)?
3. When do you want to start?
4. Is this action tied to a deadline?

How extensive has your action plan become? Is it realistic or too much of a good thing?

Action Plan for Self-Management

What?	Who?	Starting When?	Until When?	Control

The problem with action plans is that we usually begin by tackling too much, and that over time these well-intended efforts to improve and change our work habits will fade away. The contract in the beginning of this book was meant to show you how important it is to the author that you not fall victim to this problem after reading the book. The following contract with yourself should help you, after you've finished this book, transfer the self-management techniques into practice.

7.2   MAKING A CONTRACT WITH YOURSELF

This contract should help you change your perspectives, attitudes, and feelings. You can make this contract with regard to yourself, your staff, your boss, and/or your private life.

Take your time and try to answer the following questions. Reflect on the real and imagined advantages of your old work habits. If you hadn't seen some advantages in these old habits, you wouldn't have developed them in the first place. What, for example, is the advantage in your being able to say that you're constantly on the road, totally overworked, or never have any time? Are you looking for admiration or attention?

Contract with Myself   **Date:** _____

1. What do I really want to change? (Be as precise as possible.)

2. What do I want to avoid in the future?

3. What advantages did I gain from my old attitudes and work habits?

4. How can I retain these advantages with different attitudes and different work habits?

Contract with Myself—*Concluded*

---

5. What do I have to do specifically to achieve this goal? In which situations can I test the changes?

6. How can others tell that I have changed?

7. How will I try to deceive myself in order not to fulfill the contract?

8. What outside difficulties are to be expected? How can I confront these difficulties?

9. Deadline for the first control point to see whether I have kept the contract (two to four weeks).

10. How well did I fulfill my contract? (Ask these questions after every deadline.) If I didn't fulfill the contract, what were the reasons?

_____

Signature

7.3 TIPS FOR PUTTING THEORY INTO PRACTICE

The problem with self-management is not usually an inadequate knowledge of the methods, but an inadequate application of them. Here are some tips:

1. Check out each method, for example, "Do first things first"—even if it sounds trivial. Why not try it?

2. Start with a problem that is really important to you. Here again use the principle of setting priorities. Focus all your energy on this problem, for example, by organizing daily plans with the five-step-method.

3. Don't try to be perfect. Initiate only actions that can be realized: good is better than perfect.

4. Don't start actions that look reasonable from an objective point of view, but where there is emotional resistance on your part. It might look reasonable to you to jog at six o'clock every morning. But if you're a passionate late riser, the chance for permanently realizing this action is fairly low.

5. Start each activity as intensively as possible. In the beginning avoid long breaks and monitor yourself with a checklist that you use daily or weekly. A positive side effect of this is that you'll regularly have a sense of achievement.

6. For your first action plan, tackle only one big action and a few smaller ones and finish them first, before—encouraged by success—you tackle the next activities.

7. Decide for yourself whether you want to announce your changes and involve other people in helping you succeed, or if you want to tackle certain problems without others knowing about it.

8. Have someone else put pressure on you; for example, get your secretary to remind you and monitor you.

9. Talk to your staff about your intentions and try to involve them.

10. Don't tackle too much at one time. Set realistic deadlines and break your activity down into manageable steps.

11. Check your progress from time to time. Also check the usefulness of the new self-management methods. Keep in mind that you can start every day. In the end it won't count what you've started, but what you've successfully accomplished.

12. Monitor your actions on a timely basis so that there is still time for corrections.

7.4   AVOIDANCE STRATEGIES
AND RESISTANCE

Only *you* can change your attitude; others can only motivate or
hinder you. On the other hand, you may be your own worst
enemy. Therefore, we would like you to participate in the following creative exercise that has proven effective in seminars:

Transfer Exercise
How can I avoid being successful?

1.
2.
3.
4.
5.
6.
7.
8.
9.
10.

Here is a sample of answers given by seminar participants:

• No planning
• Spending too much time planning
• Planning each and every thing (perfectionism)
• Setting unrealistic deadlines for activities
• Ignoring entries in the time planner
• Imprecise defining of tasks
• Not checking up on task completion
• Not deferring unfinished tasks
• Neglecting priorities
• Setting wrong priorities
• Accepting new tasks indiscriminately (can't say no)
• Accepting deadlines without careful calculations
• Having no self-control or self-discipline
• Being an easy prey to interruptions

- Having a negative attitude toward time-planning techniques and having no motivation
- Failing to make staff and colleagues play by the rules
- Not reprimanding staff members when needed
- Sloppily executing plans
- Not learning from planning mistakes

Avoidance Strategies and Resistance. How will you try to deceive yourself not to work systematically, for example, when an unpleasant task has the highest priority?

- Are you going to open the mail first?
- Are you going to have a distracting conversation with somebody?
- Are you going to take a look into the newspaper or the latest issue of a business magazine?
- Are you going to start with a less important or easier task?
- Are you going to clean up your desk or office?
- Are you going to make a few quick phone calls?
- _____? (Your version)

Or are you going to try to build up resistance against the very idea of self-management?

- I've never done it that way.
- I've been doing something similar for years.
- With my job as . . . it won't work.
- My colleagues (boss or staff) will laugh at me.
- The hectic pace, the daily pressure, and the deadlines don't leave time for that.
- It works only in theory.
- These are all truisms.
- If it were that simple, everybody would do it.

Maybe you'll try one or several of the self-management techniques. Try to find out what methods or styles suit you personally, and improve on them continually. There is always an easier way of doing things.
Good luck!

7.5   EXERCISE

Instead of the usual summary, you'll find a final exercise on this page. Fill in your action plan based on the single most important principle, which is to *set your priorities*.

Transferring: How to Put Theory into Practice

Most Important Actions

A. _____

A. _____

A. _____

A. _____

A. _____

Important Actions

B. _____

B. _____

B. _____

B. _____

B. _____

Less Important Actions

C. _____

C. _____

C. _____

C. _____

C. _____

WORKS IN ENGLISH ABOUT
TIME MANAGEMENT

Bliss, Edwin C. *Getting Things Done: The ABCs of Time Management.* New York: Bantam Books, 1980.
———. *Doing It Now: A Twelve-Step Program for Curing Procrastination and Achieving Your Goals.* Toronto, 1983.
Davidson, Jim. *Effective Time Management.* New York: Human Sciences Press, 1978.
Douglass, Merrill E., and Donna N. Douglass. *Manage Your Time, Manage Your Work, Manage Yourself.* New York: AMACOM, 1980.
Doyle, Michael, and David Straus. *How to Make Meetings Work: The New Interaction Method.* New York: Jove Publication, 1982.
Drucker, Peter F. *The Effective Executive.* London: W. Heinemann, 1982.
Ellis, Albert, and William J. Knaus. *Overcoming Procrastination: How to Think and Act Rationally in Spite of Life's Inevitable Hassles.* New York: New American Library, 1977.
Fanning, Tony, and Robbie Fanning. *Get it All Done and Still Be Human: A Personal Time-Management Workshop.* New York: Ballantine Books, 1985.
Ferner, Jack D. *Successful Time Management: A Self-Teaching Guide.* New York: John Wiley & Sons, 1980.
Hobbs, Charles R. *Your Time and Your Life: The Insight System for Planning* (audiocassette). Chicago: Nightingale-Conant, 1983.
Holland, Gary. *Running a Business Meeting.* New York: Dell Trade, 1984.
Januz, Lauren R., and Susan K. Jones. *Time-Management for Executives: A Handbook* from the Editors of ExecuTime. New York: Charles Scribner's Sons, 1981.

Komar, John J. *The Great Escape from Your Dead-end Job*. Chicago: Follett Publishing, 1980.

Lakein, Alan. *How to Get Control of Your time and Your Life*. New York: New American Library, 1974.

LeBoeuf, Michael. *Working Smart: How to Accomplish More in Half the Time*. New York: Warner Press, 1980.

Lockett, John. *Be the Most Effective Manager in Your Business*. Rochester, N.Y.: Thorsons Publishing, 1987.

Love, Sidney F. *Mastery and Management of Time*. Englewood Cliffs, N.J.: Prentice-Hall, 1978.

Mackenzie, R. Alec. *The Time Trap: How to Get More Done in Less Time*. New York: McGraw-Hill, 1975.

McCay, James: *The Management of Time*. Englewood Cliffs, N.J.: Prentice-Hall, 1973.

McGee-Cooper, Ann. *Time Management for Unmanageable People*. Dallas, Tex.: McGee-Cooper Enterprises, 1983.

Moskowitz, Robert. *How to Organize Your Work and Your Life: Proven Time Management Techniques for Business, Professional, and Other Busy People*. Garden City, N.Y.: Doubleday, 1981.

Noon, James. *Time for Success?* London: Thomson Publishing, 1983.

————. *"A" Time: The Busy Manager's Action Plan for Effective Self Management*. Wokingham, United Kingdom, Van Nostrand Reinhold, 1985.

Oncken, Jr., William. *Managing Management Time: Who's Got the Monkey?* Englewood Cliffs, N.J.: Prentice-Hall, 1984.

Pedler, Mike; John Burgoyne; and Tom Boydell. *A Manager's Guide to Self-Development*. London: McGraw-Hill, 1978.

Reynolds, Helen, and Mary E. Tramel. *Executive Time Management: Getting 12 Hours' Work out of an 8-Hour Day*. Englewood Cliffs, N.J.: Prentice-Hall, 1979.

Scharf, Diana, and Pam Hait. *Studying Smart: Time Management for College Students*. New York: Barnes & Noble, 1985.

Scott, Dru. *How to Put More Time in Your Life*. New York: New American Library, 1981.

Sloma, Richard S. *No-Nonsense Management: A General Manager's Primer.* New York: Bantam Books, 1981.

Taylor, Harold L. *Making Time Work for You: A Guide Book to Effective & Productive Time Management*. Toronto: General Publishing, 1981.

————. *Delegate: The Key to Successful Management*. Toronto: General Publishing, 1984.

Turla, Peter, and Kathleen Hawkins. *Time Management Made Easy.* New York: E. P. Dutton, 1983.

Webber, Ross A. *A Guide to Getting Things Done* (originally published as *Time Is Money! The Key to Managerial Success*). New York: Free Press, 1980.

Winston, Stephanie. *Getting Organized.* Part I, *Time and Paperwork.* New York: Warner Press, 1980.

INDEX

A

ABC analysis for priorities, 82–86
Abilities
  analyzing, 35–37
  profile, 38
Action plan for self-management,
    208–9, 214
Activities, planned versus un-
    planned, 50; see also Daily
    activities
Agendas
  goals for, 166
  time estimates for, 166
Analysis of Time and Activities
    Form, 139–41
Answering machines, 182, 184–85
ASAP pitfalls, 53

B

Biorhythms
  caution days, 123, 125
  cautions regarding, 125–26
  elements in, 124
  sensitivity to, 125
  theory of, 121
  types, 121–22
  uses for, 125–26
Breaks
  importance of, 110
  length for, 110
  timing for, 110
Bureauglyphics, 69

C

Checklists
  advantages of, 199
  conference, 10
  development of, 199–201
  uses for, 198–99
Communication, 12–13; see also
    Information
Commuting time, 71
Concentration
  fostering of, 114, 173
  interference with, 153
  productivity and, 114
Conference checklists, 10
Controlling
  aids to, 139
  daily routines, 139
  methods for, 138
  outcome versus process, 142
  reasons behind, 137–38
Control list, 143
Correspondence
  dictating, 198
  efficiency in, 193–98
  incoming, 193–94
    acting on, 194
    immediate replies to, 194–95
    marking of, 193–94
    presorted, 193
  outgoing, 194–98
    computer-generated, 197
    form letters for, 196–97
    letter copies for, 195

Correspondence—*Con't.*
 personalized, 197–98
 quick response to, 195–96
 redi-letters for, 195–96

D

Daily activities; *see also* Task lists
  and Time planning
 breaks within, 110
 consequences of, 141
 controlling, 139
 evaluation of, 143–44
 grouping, 111–12
 high point in, 115–16
 organizing, 105–6, 132–34
 personal rhythms and, 12, 118;
  see also Productivity curve
 plan adjustments, 107
 planning, 115
 predictable disturbances, 113–14
 review of, 143
 unplanned, 110
 weeding, 109
 winding up, 115
Daily Plan
 example, 68
 form, 64
 graphic symbols in, 69
Deadlines
 importance of, 52–53
 mini contracts for, 53
 negotiating, 109
 realistic, 211
 working around, 48
Decision making
 importance of, 79–81
 time loss in, 11
Delegation
 benefits of, 88–90
 choosing tasks for, 94–95
 from daily task list, 67
 defined, 88
 five-step method, 97

Delegation—*Con't.*
 follow-up, 97–99
 importance of, 53
 practicing, 48
 resistance to, 90–92
 of responsibility, 88
 rules of, 93–94, 96–98
 six W rules, 98
 style of, 92
 and task value, 84–85
 of telephone calls, 186
 time frame for, 95
 vertical versus horizontal, 95–96
Dialog Preparation Form, 174–75
Dictation efficiency, 198
Distraction sources, 8
Disturbances
 analysis, 10
 controlling, 141
 cycles of, 113–14

E

80:20 Rule, 81–82
Eisenhower principle for setting
  priorities, 86–88
Ends/means analysis, 39
Excerpts
 advantages of, 156
 files of, 161
 format, 161
 form for, 158
 importance of, 163
 key-word, 161
 paraphrased, 157
 photocopying for, 157
 structural, 159
 summarized, 157
 tape recorded, 161
 topic summary, 160–161
 verbatim, 156
 view, 161
 visual memory and, 159

F–G

Failures, personal, 37
Form letters, 196–97
Free time
    planning, 54
    uses for, 4–5
Goals
    action-oriented, 25, 42
    deadlines for, 40–42, 55–62
    development of, 1
    ends/means analysis, 39
    professional, 30
    selectivity in, 40
    short-term versus long-term, 40
Goal setting
    analysis, 42
    benefits of, 22–23
    method, 24
    nature of, 22–23
    need for, 24
    process, 38
    written, 25

H–I

Höhn, R., 63
Hummel, Charles E., 53
Ideals
    establishing, 26–28
    evaluation, 31
    professional, 31
    ranking, 28
Information
    excerpting, 156–61
    gleaning methods, 149–52, 155–63
    goal-relevant, 147
    overload, 147
    processing, 147
    as time waster, 149
Interruptions; see also Telephone
        calls and Visitors
    analysis, 10
    avoidance of, 112–13, 173

Interruptions—Con't.
    scheduling against, 114
    sources, 8

K–L

Killer phrases, 166
Lee, Ivy, 79
Letter copies, 195
Life curve recording, 26–27

M–O

Mackenzie, R.A., 80
Management style, staff-oriented,
        172
Marcoglyphics, 155
Marking techniques
    symbols for, 155–56
    use of, 163
Meetings
    alternatives to, 165
    avoiding, 165
    checklist for, 167
    concluding, 168
    cost-benefit analysis, 164
    efficiency in, 164–70
    goals for, 166
    handling of, 166, 168–69
    locations for, 173
    minutes, 169–71
    participant selection, 165
    participant types, 168–69
    preparation checklist, 199
    situations requiring, 165
    with staff, 173
    structure for, 166
Mini contracts for deadlines, 53
Minutes
    form for, 171
    importance of, 169
    instant, 170
    of meetings, 169–70
    telephone calls, 191–93

Objectives
  inventory, 32–33
  precisely defined, 25
  setting, 11
  steps in establishing, 26
  time chart, 28–30
Overwork as symptom, 1

P–Q

Pareto time principle, 81
Perfectionism, 211
Peripheral reading, 155
Personal habits
  productivity and, 118
  work performance and, 106–7
Positive attitude, 106, 115, 212
Priorities
  immediacy versus importance in,
    87
  methods of establishing, 81–88
Productivity
  concentration and, 114
  obstacles to, 127–28
  over time, 111
Productivity curve
  nature of, 116–17
  personal assessment, 119–20
  work quality and, 120
Promotions forcasting, 41
Quick reply method, 194–95
Quiet hour
  need for, 114
  visitors and, 173

R

Reading; *see also* Excerpts
  bad habits, 152–53
  diagonally, 153–54
  efficiency in, 148
  goal-oriented, 151–53
  improvement, 151–53
  with a marker, 155
  memorizing while, 162

Reading—*Con't.*
  peripheral, 155
  purposes of, 163
  questioning while, 162–63
  scheduling, 149
  selective, 148–49
  slalom technique, 154
  speed, 148, 152–55
  SQ 3R method, 148, 162–63
  strategies, 149–55, 162
Reddin, William J., 2
Redi-letters, 195–96
Robinson, F., 148, 162

S

Schwab, Charles M., 79–80
Secretaries
  letter-writing by, 198
  morning conference with, 108
  phone call screening by, 182–84
  phone dialing by, 186–87
  visitor handling through, 177
  visitor screening by, 173–74
Self-control versus other-control, 1,
    137; *see also* Controlling
Self-management
  action plan for, 208–9, 214
  advantages, 3–4
  aids to, 114–15
  contract, 20
  control and, 137
  decision-making, 79
  defined, 1
  failure in, 212–13
  functional diagram, 15–26
  need for, 1
  process control, 142
  resistance to, 213
  self-contract, 209–10
  self-evaluation, 3
  setting priorities for, 100
  tehniques, 16–17
  theory into practice, 210–14
Situation analysis
  personal, 33–34

Situation analysis—*Con't.*
  professional, 34–35
  steps in, 33
60:40 rule 49, 68
Slalom technique, 154
SQ 3R method, 148, 162–63
Staff
  conversation strategies, 176
  meetings with, 173, 176
  written communication by, 176
Stress
  decreasing, 49
  as a symptom, 1
  work pace and, 111
Success
  accidental versus planned, 23–24
  keys to, 31
  personal, 35–37
  professional, 35

T

Task lists
  ABC analysis for, 82–86
  construction, 64–65
  pressing items, 109–10
  priorities in, 80–88
  re-evaluation, 130–32
  recurring tasks, 201
  strategies for, 213
  time horizons, 66
  weeding, 67
Telephone calls
  advantages of, 179, 181
  avoidance strategies, 182–85
  call back strategy, 185
  concluding, 191
  delegating, 186
  documenting, 191–93
  efficiency in, 180
  grouping of, 182
  incoming, 180–85
  inefficient use of, 178–79
  notes of, 191–93
  organizing, 187

Telephone calls—*Con't.*
  outgoing, 180, 185–93
  preparations, 188
  preparations checklist, 189
  priority codes for, 186
  processing checklist, 184
  screening, 181–84
  screening checklist, 183
  strategies, 190–91
  time blocks for, 186
  as time wasters, 178–79
  timing of, 187–88
  tyranny of, 178
Time analysis, positive versus negative aspects, 8–9
Time buffers
  creating, 49–50
  need for, 54
  tasks during, 114
  using, 48, 66–67
Time/Design®, Time/system®, 59, 61, 68, 85, 99, 107, 167, 202
Time frames, 52
Time loss
  analysis, 10–13
  checklist, 11–13
  sources of, 13
Time planner, 69
  versus appointment books, 72–73
  data for, 74
  format, 73–74
  index, 73
  page markers, 73
  phone call lists in, 187
Time planning
  ABC analysis and, 85
  action-oriented, 52
  advantages, 46–49, 70–71
  basics, 45–55
  corporate, 55–56
  daily, 60–72, 115
  efficiency in, 11
  five-step method, 62–64
  flexibility, 51
  focus for, 55

Time planning—*Con't.*
  free time, 54
  initiating, 71
  lack of, 1
  mini contracts, 53
  monthly, 58–59
  multiyear, 57
  quarterly, 57
  realism in, 51
  reviewing, 54
  rules of, 75–76
  system for, 55–62
  time blocks in, 54
  time horizons in, 51
  time spent in, 46–47
  variety in, 55
  weekly, 60–61
  written, 51–52, 62
  yearly, 57
Time use
  analysis, 6–10
  work sheets, 7
Time wasters
  analysis, 13–15
  productivity and, 14
  solutions to, 15, 128–30
  in work habits, 107–8
Trickett, Joseph M., 185
Tyranny of the Urgent, 53; *see also*
  Eisenhower Principle

U–V

Unconscious energy, 23
Visitors
  conversation strategies, 174–76
  getting rid of, 177–78
  management strategies, 172–78
  reasons for, 170, 172
  screening of, 172
  as time wasters, 170
  unannounced, 177

W–Z

Work blocks, 112
Work habits
  activity-oriented, 2
  analysis, 5
  efficient versus effective, 2
  goal-oriented, 2
  improving, 12, 63
  monitoring, 211
  persistence, 112–13
  questionnaire, 3
  realism in, 211
  re-evaluation, 130–32
  regularity in, 107
  self-evaluation, 126–27
  time wasters, 107–8
Work pace and stress, 111
Zielke, Wolfgang, 157

Enjoy the Benefits of a New Method of Organization

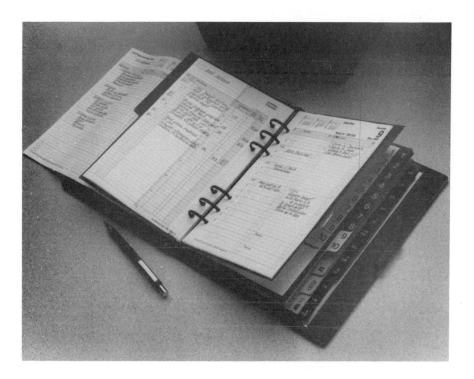